Contents

Acknowledgements

I would like to sincerely thank the following individuals and organizations who have assisted me during the writing and photographing of this book: JoAnne D. Holden-Arbing, the Prince Edward Island National Park, Parks Canada, Department of Canadian Heritage; Mel Melonson, Monique Pinkham, and Chris Diamond, Green Gables House, Cavendish, part of Prince Edward Island National Park, Parks Canada, Department of Canadian Heritage; John and Jennie Macneill, the Lucy Maud Montgomery Cavendish home site; Francis W. P. Bolger, the Lucy Maud Montgomery birthplace, New London; George and Maureen Campbell and Ruth Campbell, the Anne of Green Gables Museum at Silver Bush, Park Corner; Robert Montgomery, the Lucy Maud Montgomery Heritage Museum, Park Corner; the people of Kensington, the Kensington Train Station; the Board of Trustees and congregation of the Cavendish United Church, Cavendish; Bob Fear, the Green Gables Post Office and Heritage Museum, Cavendish; the Orwell Corner Historic Village, Orwell; and the Prince Edward Island Museum and Heritage Foundation. I would like to especially thank my editors at Nimbus Publishing Ltd., Dorothy Blythe and Liane Heller, and Arthur Carter for his design. Finally, I would like to thank my husband, Harvey, and my children, Matthew and Gina, for all their help and support.

Anne's World, Maud's World:
The Sacred Sites
of L.M. Montgomery

TEXT AND PHOTOGRAPHS:
∾ Nancy Rootland ∾

NIMBUS
PUBLISHING LTD

Nimbus Publishing Limited
P.O. Box 9301, Station A
Halifax, Nova Scotia B3K 5N5
(902) 455-4286

Design: Arthur B. Carter, Halifax, NS
Literary Editor: Liane Heller, Halifax, NS
Printed and bound in Hong Kong By
Everbest Printing Co. Ltd.

Canadian Cataloguing in Publication Data
Rootland, Nancy.
Anne's world, Maud's world
Includes bibliographical references.
ISBN 1-55109-142-9
1. Montgomery, L.M. (Lucy Maud), 1874-1942—Homes and
haunts. 2. Montgomery, L.M. (Lucy Maud), 1874-1942—
Homes and haunts—Pictorial works. 3. Shirley, Anne
(Fictitious character). 4. Prince Edward Island—Pictorial
works. 5. Prince Edward Island—Description and travel.
6. Literary landmarks—Prince Edward Island—Pictorial
works. I. Title.
PS8526.055Z85 1996   C813'.52   C95-950320X
PR9199.2.M66Z85 1996

98 99 4 3 2

Front cover: Green Gables House. A Cavendish landmark for decades, this frame
house provides the setting for Anne of Green Gables. It is also a real home, built
in the mid-1800s and once owned by relatives of the author.

Back cover: Site of Montgomery's maternal grandparents' home, where Maud
grew to womanhood.

Title page: Lucy Maud Montgomery at about age twenty-one. As a child she
explored every corner of Balsam Hollow, a lush grove of evergreens near the
"real" Green Gables on which she based the home of her fictional alter ego
Anne Shirley. Portrait courtesy of Prince Edward Island National Park.

To the memory of my Grandmother and Grandfather

Green Gables, stark white against a deep blue
sky with roof and gables a sharp vivid green.

INTRODUCTION

In January of 1981, I was browsing in a bookstore in Southern California when the title *Anne of Green Gables* caught my eye. Maybe it was the sound of those words that drew me in—fresh, inviting, intriguing—or the image of a lonely child sitting on a train platform. I slid the book off the shelf and started leafing through the pages—and that was it. I could barely put it down long enough to get over to the sales desk, and while I was driving home my eyes kept wandering over to the package on the seat next to me.

I raced through the book in one sitting, astounded at how Anne Shirley's experiences mirrored my own. Like Anne, I had been a sensitive child, steeped in fairy tales and mythology; like Anne, I spent my days exploring the natural wonders of my world; like Anne, I had a best friend—a "kindred spirit"—and like Anne, I am a Pisces: imaginative, creative, intuitive.

Then there was the writing, so evocative, so highly visual that all of Anne's special places—like Lovers' Lane and the Lake of Shining Waters—came alive for me, in that inexplicable way that a book has with a willing reader. In her language resided all the colours, shapes, and sounds of a sun-streaked, rippling, gently gurgling brook in the leafy enclosure of a spruce grove; all the terrors of the rustling, skeletal, spectral trees in the Haunted Wood.

Lucy Maud Montgomery's words spoke to me—and fourteen years later, they still do—as no other author's ever have. Not only were the experiences of the major characters parallel to my own, so was Montgomery's perception of nature. My spiritual life is rooted in the natural world, and here was a writer to whom nature, and its sacred places, represented the essence of the soul. I remember places like that in my grandfather's gardens; the fields, ponds, and canals near my home; and the pine forests of my Girl scouting days—places that time cannot change—but I never expected to find them in the words of an author from faraway Prince Edward Island. And I never expected them to make such a deep and lasting impression.

The interiors of the novel, too, were places made sacred by the people who inhabited them, and whose thoughts and deeds illuminated them. Matthew's corner by the kitchen stove, where the good-hearted guardian of Anne (along with his sister, Marilla) sits dreaming over his pipe about a stylish new dress for the child's Christmas present. The Green Gables sitting-room, glowing in the afternoon light that streams through the blossoming apple trees onto the motionless figure of Anne as she stares raptly at the painting called "Christ Blessing Little Children." Or the parlour at Anne's friend Diana's house, where the very best china is laden with "fruit-cake and dough-nuts and two kinds of preserves" to honour Anne for saving the life of her best friend's baby sister.

In fact, to such an extent were these places a portrayal of the spirit's yearning for beauty and harmony that I wondered whether they existed at all, outside the realm of Montgomery's fertile imagination. Through research I discovered that they did—the communities, beaches, forests, lanes, lakes, and ponds were real places, located on Prince Edward Island's North Shore.

Even Green Gables was authentic, a house built in the mid-1800s and once owned by elderly cousins of the author's. Only some of the names were different; for example, the Avonlea of the novel was the village of Cavendish, where Montgomery had grown up, and whose surroundings had given rise to the unforgettable descriptions that were fast turning me into a devotee. The urge to go there, to absorb that charmed geography—to experience and to record in photography and text what I was growing to love through Montgomery's descriptions—became my passion. And I had only just finished the first novel!

As it turned out, my first journey to Cavendish would have to wait eleven years. I had two young children to raise, and the demands of work and home were endless. But at least I could make time to delve into the rest of Montgomery's writings. By the end of the summer I had read all twenty novels; any that I could not find on the shelves at my local library were ordered in from branches all over the state. And through the University of California, Riverside, I discovered a collection of letters written by Montgomery from 1903-1941, published in *My Dear Mr. M: Letters to G.B. MacMillan*. In 1985 I was able to obtain the first volume of her journals; the second in 1987.

Slowly, and with an increasing awareness of our shared sensibility, I began to understand the life of this extraordinary woman, the natural and emotional forces that shaped her childhood and youth, and, most importantly, the crucial roles played by the characters and places in the *Anne* books in allowing Montgomery to fully express the emotional scope of her inner life—and share this bounty with us.

∽

Lovers' Lane, Lucy Maud Montgomery's name—Anne Shirley's, too—for the pathway that starts just below the orchard at Green Gables. It's either the way to get cows to and from pasture, or a place of wonder, depending on your point of view. And sometimes it's both.

Lucy Maud Montgomery was born November 30, 1874, the only child of Clara Woolner Macneill and Hugh John Montgomery. Her birthplace, the village of Clifton, P.E.I. (now better known as New London), and in particular the tiny house where her parents moved soon after their marriage, would become one of young Maud's most beloved sacred places. Sadly, she would not live there long. She was barely a year old when she and her mother, gravely ill with tuberculosis—the dreaded "consumption"—moved into the Cavendish home of Clara's parents, Alexander and Lucy Macneill. But as Maud grew, the site of her birth became an enchanted place within her mind. She could not travel past the little house at the crossroads without thinking of what once was, and what might have been.

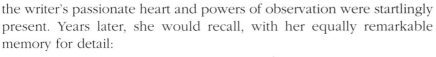

"That one precious memory is all I have of a girlish mother who sleeps in the old burying-ground of Cavendish, lulled forever by the murmur of the sea."

Maud was not yet two years old when her mother died, but already the writer's passionate heart and powers of observation were startlingly present. Years later, she would recall, with her equally remarkable memory for detail:

My father was standing by the casket holding me in his arms. I wore a little white muslin dress and Father was crying....I looked down at Mother's dead face. It was a sweet little face, albeit worn by months of suffering. My mother had been beautiful, and Death, so cruel in all else, had spared the delicate outline of feature, the long silken lashes brushing the hollow cheeks, and the smooth masses of golden brown hair....I reached down and laid my baby hand against that cheek. Even now I can feel the coldness of that touch....

—"The Alpine Path," *Everywoman's World*, June 1917

But there could not have been any conception of death for a child so young—only the chilling knowledge that something was terribly wrong. Everything had changed and nothing would ever be the same.

Following Clara's death, Hugh John Montgomery left Maud with her maternal grandparents, to be raised in the Macneill homestead. And although Hugh spent some time in Cavendish after his wife's death, he accepted work in Prince Albert, Saskatchewan, and moved out west permanently when Maud was seven, leaving her to stay on with her grandparents. Already in their mid-fifties when Maud first came to live with them, Alexander and Lucy Macneill had already raised six children, and were, to say the least, set in their ways. Young Maud's sensitive, emotional nature shrank from the repressive atmosphere of the household—rules about everything from how she wore her hair to who her friends should be—and from the coldness of her grandparents.

Not that they were cruel—Maud had the best of everything when it came to material necessities, and as the Macneills were extremely fond of literature, they encouraged their granddaughter to help herself to the leather-bound volumes in the big bookshelves. Poetry was predominant in the Macneill library—the family had produced several poets—and even before she started school, Maud was devouring the complex creations of Longfellow, Scott, Byron, Whittier, Milton, and Burns.

There's no doubt that the Macneills cared deeply for Maud, expressing their regard as best they knew how, but their rigid discipline drove her deep within herself. She invented imaginary playmates to fill the void; trees and flowers, too, became her friends, each with a name and story to suit its "personality." Her grandparents had no objection to her spending plenty of time outdoors in the fresh air, so the fields, brooks, dunes, and sea of Cavendish became the setting for her world of imagination—a world where her spirit could roam free. A world where she could just be!

It was not an entirely solitary childhood. Maud looked forward to spending time with her father and especially enjoyed travelling with

Young Maud treasured her visits to the Park Corner home of her beloved Grandfather Montgomery—especially if her father was home for a visit and could accompany her.

him to nearby Park Corner to visit her paternal grandparents and play with her cousins, the Campbells, who lived in the farmhouse just across from the Montgomerys. Grandfather Montgomery recognized and appreciated Maud's sensitivity and was particularly kind to her; and she recalled the Campbell house as always being full of joy and laughter. Even at home, Maud found some solace in a close relationship with her Aunt Emily, the youngest of the Macneill daughters; still a very young woman when Maud arrived, she grew to become almost a surrogate mother to the little girl.

But the relative stability that had slowly built up after her mother's death was shaken when Maud's father took a permant job in Saskatchewan. Around the same time, her Aunt Emily was married and she too moved away. Luckily, these severe blows to Maud's already unsteady sense of emotional equilibrium were not fatal. The years that followed brought new people, and a new feeling of belonging, to her life. Wellington and David Nelson, two children of Maud's age who lived too far from Cavendish school to travel there daily, came to board with the Macneills. The three became fast friends, exploring the coastline, tending their small garden, and building a playhouse that became their favourite refuge.

At school, although her friendships were limited by her grandparents' exacting standards of suitable companionship, Maud was able to find not only a friend, but a best friend, Amanda Macneill. Penzie Macneill,

The tree-lined path from the Macneill property to Cavendish school seemed a much brighter place to Maud when the Nelson boys came to board with her grandparents.

three years her elder, was also deemed an appropriate playmate: Amanda and Penzie were also Maud's cousins.

But relationships with children other than those few, sanctioned by her grandparents, were limited to school hours. The Macneills insisted that Maud return home at noon for dinner each day, and although the Nelson boys' arrival meant she was no longer the only one separated from her friends—and their noontime laughter and games—she still felt the sting, and the stigma, of being somehow different from the others. By the tender age of eight, Maud had endured more than her share of sorrow: her mother's death, and her father's distant relocation. The pain of this double loss, along with the strictness of her upbringing, gave her inner life a dark side that contrasted sharply with the experiences of the fun-loving girl who, with her friends, "had some dandy old times together, coasting and berrying and picking gum and going to the shore and playing with the cats in the barn," as Montgomery wrote in her journals.

❧

Self-expression through art is a liberating experience. The imaginings, longings, hopes, sorrows, and fears to which we can't give voice in our everyday lives are encouraged to flourish in creative endeavours, transforming both audience and artist. In the work of few writers that I know does this process flourish more than in the books of Lucy Maud Montgomery.

Ever since Maud could remember, she dreamed of being a writer, keeping a diary that faithfully and meticulously described her thoughts, feelings, impressions, and experiences. Old "letter bills"—forms used for inter-office transfers within the postal system—discarded from the Cavendish post office (located in the Macneill kitchen) provided a steady supply of paper; and her active imagination, flair for words, and sensitive heart inspired a steady flow of journal entries, poems, and, later, essays and stories. The school collection of children's literature opened up a whole new world to a six-year-old who had already been reading and writing for some time, and her classes gave Maud an even greater opportunity for creative expression, through writing or in reciting her favourite poems and dialogues.

But her acute sensitivity, and the indifference others often displayed towards it, affected her early development as a writer. She was only nine years old when she wrote her first poem, "Autumn," which she proudly recited to her father when he came back to the Island for a visit. His reaction, that it "didn't sound much like poetry," hurt Maud deeply; and when she haltingly tried to explain that the piece was not in rhyming couplets but in blank verse, he replied that it was "very blank indeed." Not even this thoughtless rejoinder could stop Maud from writing—nothing could—but she did become more protective about sharing her work; years would go by before she actively sought any outside commentary on her writing.

As she grew older, and her need for outside reaction to her work intensified, she found ingenious ways of eliciting opinions without opening herself to the hurt they might cause.

She wanted desperately to recite one of her poems to her teacher, Izzie Robinson, but knew the woman could be very critical. Miss Robinson, who boarded at the Macneills' for a time, resented Grandfather Macneill's characteristic sarcasm and apparently took out her feelings on Maud by regularly humiliating her in class. As she recalled in her journals, Maud hit on the idea of introducing her poem, "Evening Dreams," as a song lyric; Miss Robinson responded that she was unfamiliar with it, "but the words were pretty"—praise that was bittersweet, as she had to become anonymous to earn it.

Later, a more sympathetic teacher, and the encouragement of seeing her poems and short stories published in newspapers and magazines, helped ease the sting. But Maud never forgot those hurtful incidents surrounding her budding literary ambitions—just as she never forgot the pain she felt when adults laughed at the sophisticated vocabulary she used, even as a very young child. Such memories found their way into her novels: "It's nicer to think dear, pretty thoughts and keep them in one's heart, like treasures," muses the young heroine of *Anne of Green Gables*. "I don't like to have them laughed at or wondered over." Indeed, all her recollections, joyful as well as unpleasant, flowed into her books.

Maud was thirty-two and had worked as a teacher, journalist, and assistant postmistress to her grandmother when *Anne* was finally accepted for publication by L.C. Page of Boston. She had also been a published writer for half her life. But she had, in a sense, been writing *Anne* all her life, drawing on every noteworthy experience, each memorable person, and, especially, all the places, wondrous and beautiful, haunting and intimidating—whether the cool recesses of a house, the grand sweep of the sea, the glittering greenness of a sunlit, tree-lined path, or the light-filled interior of a one-room schoolhouse with its "comfortable substantial old-fashioned desks."

The parallels between characters and locations in *Anne* and the details of Maud's own life are innumerable, and the most significant is that of author to protagonist. Anne arrives in Avonlea an orphan, different from other children in her wonderfully active imagination, love of books, and predilection for "big words"; Maud had lost her mother and been separated from her father, and she, like her fictional alter ego, stood out from her peers because of her intense attraction to the life of the mind. Like Anne, Maud felt the constraints of a household's rigid rules, although in the novel she rewrote her own history closer to her heart's desire by having Anne join her classmates for their lunchtime sojourn in the wooded hollow near the school—a pleasure the creator never enjoyed.

Most of all, both character and author shared a belief in the power of dreams—dreams that transformed everyday reality into an enchanted place where a road becomes the White Way of Delight, a pool in a neighbour's field is romantically christened Willowmere, a reflection in the glass of a china cabinet turns into a secret friend, Katie Maurice, and even a simple geranium wins the heartwarming name of Bonny. In this world, there aren't so much rocks on a beach as "little sandy coves inlaid with pebbles as with ocean jewels." Fall, more than just a season, is a magical time when "the wild cherry-trees along the lane put on the loveliest shades of dark red and bronzy green." And on a summer's night, "wind and stars and fireflies [are] all tangled up together into something unutterably sweet and enchanting."

The heritage post office in Cavendish is similar to the one at the Macneill house, where Maud helped her grandmother fulfil her duties as postmistress after the death of Grandfather Macneill.

Secondary characters, too, are drawn from Maud's life—Anne's best friend, Diana Barry, combines elements of Penzie and Amanda, in particular Amanda. The helpful teacher Miss Stacy strongly resembles Maud's favourite schoolmistress, Miss Gordon—an early champion of her gifted student's literary efforts. The stormy relationship between Anne and Gilbert faithfully echoes Maud's affections for (and competitiveness with) Nate Lockhart, stepson of the Baptist minister in Canvendish.

And Anne's adoptive guardians, Matthew and Marilla, exemplify both positive and negative characteristics of the adults in young Maud's life: the gentle sweetness of Grandfather Montgomery and Uncle John Campbell, and the stern discipline of Grandfather and Grandmother Macneill. That even the practical and unromantic Marilla comes to acknowledge early on in *Anne* that she's "getting fond of her"—and that the fondness soon grows into love—gives us all hope for the possibility that we can be transformed through deep feeling. Although Anne feels unwanted upon her arrival at Green Gables—especially by Marilla—she comes to treasure her new home, and the love within. There is no question that she will give up college to stay home and teach, rather than see Marilla forced to sell Green Gables after Matthew's death and the onset of her own failing eyesight.

Similarly, Maud decided to change her own plans after the death of her grandfather. If she had gone, Grandmother Macneill would have had to leave the old homestead. The farm had been willed to her second son, John, with the stipulation that she would be able to remain in the house until her death; but she was too old to stay there alone and look after the post office. And if Maud had not stayed on, *Anne* might never been written; for it was at the Macneill homestead that the maturing writer found the time to devote herself to her first book, as well as her short fiction and essays. Maud frequently credited her grandparents for influencing her literary career, and despite their repressiveness she expressed a deep regard for them.

Maud used her impressions of the furnishings at her grandparents' house to create the interiors of *Anne of Green Gables*. The ornamental scarf on the mantel is called a lambrequin.

ꭥ

As the years passed, I returned to Montgomery's books again and again, increasingly drawn to explore the world from which they arose. Just as my daughter was making plans to leave home for her senior year of college, I realized it was finally time for me to make what had become a pilgrimage—to Cavendish, Prince Edward Island. It was the summer of 1992; significantly, the fiftieth anniversary of Montgomery's death.

I've returned twice since then, each time taking more photographs and absorbing in more detail the wondrously beautiful setting of *Anne of Green Gables* and of its author's remarkable life. Along with Cavendish, I've visited New London, Park Corner, and other villages important to the life and work of Montgomery. Everywhere I have been fortunate to find striking reminders of the sanctity of place—and of the human spirit— so abundant in Maud, and in her beloved Anne.

ꭥ

Only a trail and a dirt road mark the spot
that used to be the bustling Hunter River
train station—the model for the Bright
River station, where Anne arrives from the
orphanage.

ANNE'S WORLD

Arrival

The Hunter River Station is no more. A bicycle trail extends through the wildflowers and coarse grass, where the tracks once ran and the station-house stood. Down the wider dirt road beside the trail, a big barnboard building, unromantically signposted PURINA CHOWS, looms over the deserted clearing.

Trains have not come through this tiny Prince Edward Island community since the CNR ceased operations on the Island in 1986; visitors to nearby Cavendish drive in, or take the bus, and they probably would never have occasion to come here, unless—

Unless they were coming to meet someone who has been waiting here for a long time. Imagine a little girl, sitting on a pile of shingles at the end of a long platform over which hangs the sign BRIGHT RIVER. An orphan, expecting to find a real home in nearby Avonlea. An orphan named Anne Shirley— eleven years old, with thick red braids, a narrow, freckled face, and big green-grey eyes. She gazes wistfully around the bend and wonders if she'll have to spend the night in that cherry tree there, just where the track curves out of sight. Of course, that wouldn't be *so* bad, would it?

Oh, but wait. There *is* someone coming. Listen—that's the sound of horses' hooves in the distance. It's Matthew Cuthbert, approaching the station where he's to collect the child he and his sister, Marilla, have adopted from an orphan asylum in Nova Scotia. Only he's expecting a boy...

Matthew had taken the scrawny little hand awkwardly in his; then and there he decided what to do. He could not tell this child with the glowing eyes that there had been a mistake; he would take her home and let Marilla do that. She couldn't be left at Bright River anyhow, no matter what mistake had been made, so all questions and explanations might as well be deferred until he was safely back at Green Gables.

"I'm sorry I was late," he said shyly. "Come along."

It is not difficult to shift from fact to fiction in this strangely sacred place, an abandoned railway station whose bustling predecessor was the prototype for one of the best-known and best-loved beginnings of a Canadian novel—*Anne of Green Gables*. As its young heroine continually exhorts her family and friends, we need only use our imaginations to transform the Hunter River of contemporary reality into the Bright River of Lucy Maud Montgomery's timeless tale.

And before we know it, we're travelling the eight miles back to Avonlea, sitting comfortably in the buggy beside the odd-looking, bashful, stoop-shouldered Matthew, as his sorrel mare pulls them steadily towards Green Gables.

At the same time, we're taking a second journey, through the very real places that inspired Montgomery's wonderful books—places that continue to inspire those of us who've come to explore them.

The Cavendish pond near the pathway leading to Green Gables.

Lake of Shining Waters

They had driven over the crest of a hill. Below them was a pond, looking almost like a river so long and winding was it. A bridge spanned it midway, and from there to its lower end, where an amber-hued belt of sand-hills shut it in from the dark blue gulf beyond, the water was a glory of many shifting hues—the most spiritual shadings of crocus and rose and ethereal green, with other elusive tintings for which no name has ever been found....

"I shall call it—let me see—the Lake of Shining Waters. Yes, that is the right name for it. I know because of the thrill. When I hit on a name that suits exactly it gives me a thrill...."

Like Anne, we all set great store in the right name—although not always with the same lyrical intensity of imagination. Sometimes, as Matthew did, we simply supply a correct name: "'That's Barry's pond,'" he told Anne, referring to the family of the girl who will become her best friend, Diana. Other times, we search eagerly for the source of the name's beauty.

In the case of Anne's Lake of Shining Waters, the pond on the Campbell property at Park Corner, where Maud frequently visited her Uncle John and Aunt Annie, was the inspiration for Anne's enchanted "lake." Although in her journals, Maud writes: "A good many of the effects of light and shadow I have seen on the Cavendish pond figured unconsciously in my description; and certainly the hill from which Anne caught her first glimpse of it was 'Laird's Hill,' where I have often stood at sunset, enraptured with the beautiful view of shining pond and crimson-brimmed harbour and dark blue sea." Nonetheless, in her own hand, she credits the Campbell pond as being the lake of Anne's vivid imagination.

When I first saw the Cavendish pond, glistening like a sea of diamonds in the afternoon sunlight, I was very near the pathway leading to Green Gables, and could well understand how the effects of light and shadow would have influenced Maud.

How like Anne, I thought—tranquil as a daydream, yet rippling like a laugh (and, at times, tempestuous as a summer storm!). And how like Maud, too, that combination of stillness and energy.

Later, I had the opportunity to visit Park Corner and see Campbell's pond, located on the family homestead, Silver Bush. These shining waters reflected images of young Maud whiling away a summer afternoon playing happily with her three cousins, and it was easy to understand why she thought of it when creating Anne's famous "lake."

But I suppose first impressions are strongest, and for me, the Cavendish pond will always represent that moment just before the first glimpse of home.

Path to Green Gables

*Below was a little valley, and beyond a long, gently-rising slope
with snug farmsteads scattered along it. From one to another the
child's eyes darted, eager and wistful. At last they lingered on one
away to the left, far back from the road, dimly white with blossoming trees in the twilight of the surrounding woods....*

"That's it, isn't it?" she said, pointing.

Matthew slapped the reins on the sorrel's back delightedly.

*"Well now, you've guessed it! But I reckon Mrs Spencer described
it so's you could tell."*

*"No, she didn't—really she didn't. All she said might just as
well have been about most of those other places. I hadn't any real
idea what it looked like. But just as soon as I saw it I felt it was
home. Oh, it seems as if I must be in a dream...."*

A light dust flies up from the pathway that slopes upward, towards
Green Gables, as if a horse's hooves and the wheels of a buggy had

raised it. The rolling hills, the lush green woods, the babbling brook, and the big white house are all calling out to me. Have I been here before? Or have I dreamed it?

Beyong the path stands a white picket fence where wild rose bushes line its border. Their fresh sweetness accompanies me as I approach the house, stark white against a deep blue sky, with roof and gables a sharp, vivid green. The whole house has been freshly painted; once a brownish yellow, a typical colour for homes in the author's era, it has been restored, inside and out, to reflect as accurately as possible the descriptions in the book.

The big white house seems to beckon visitors approaching Green Gables along a path that dips down from the lush landscape of rosebushes and fruit trees.

Although the afternoon is bright and sunny, whereas Anne and Matthew arrived at twilight; although I can hear the sound of a car passing below, when of course there would have been none—although it is a story that brought me—I suddenly feel as if I truly belong here. Testament, perhaps, to the refurbishing efforts, to the fact that Green Gables is no mere fictional creation but a historic house where Maud played as a child; testament, most of all, to the deep kinship I feel for her, and for the irresistible Anne.

But the feeling of warmth and security is underscored by apprehension...

By the time they arrived at the house Matthew was shrinking from the approaching revelation with an energy he did not understand. It was not of Marilla or himself he was thinking, or of the trouble this mistake was probably going to make for them, but of the child's disappointment.

Down the Hall

Two worlds collide in this narrow passage, both of them a potent blend of despair and hope, of repression and freedom.

In the formal poses of old photographs hung in this hallway can be deciphered the visual shorthand of Maud's life, its troubles and joys. Here is the author herself, about twenty-one, her parted lips and rapt expression conveying a bountiful creative spirit. Here are Maud's grandparents, the Macneills—almost impossible not to decipher from these stiff postures and tight mouths the rigidity and coldness they imposed on the motherless child who came into their care; and yet it was their strong literary influence that led her to become an author. Here, too, are her parents—her father who clearly loved her and saw to it that she enjoyed frequent trips to Park Corner, but who left her behind for a new life on the prairies; and her mother, cruelly wrenched away when Maud was only twenty-one months old, yet alive within her as a lifelong memory of the deepest love she could imagine.

The hallway also marks the troubled beginnings of Anne's new life

in Avonlea. Standing at the bottom of the stairs, I have a clear recollection of Anne's arrival.

> *Dropping her precious carpet-bag she sprang forward a step and clasped her hands.*
>
> *"You don't want me!" she cried. "You don't want me because I'm not a boy! I might have expected it. Nobody ever did want me. I might have known it was all too beautiful to last. I might have known nobody really did want me. Oh, what shall I do? I'm going to burst into tears!"*
>
> *Burst into tears she did.*

Feelings of compassion overwhelm me, and I have a strong desire to run into the kitchen to comfort the heartbroken child. As I search for a distraction, my eyes drift up along the steep, shining, dark staircase—to where?—the old typewriter on the lamplit hall table seems to spring into view. This machine is very much like the one Maud used to compose her books, including *Anne of Green Gables,* and the choice of location provides a perfect metaphor for Anne's unsettling arrival at the house she desperately longs to call home, but cannot.

Could Maud ever truly think of the Macneills' as *home?*

> *"If I was very beautiful and had nut-brown hair would you keep me?"*
>
> *"No. We want a boy to help Matthew on the farm. A girl would be of no use to us. Take off your hat. I'll lay it and your bag on the hall table."*
>
> *Anne took off her hat meekly. Matthew came back presently and they sat down to supper.*

The Depths of Despair

Fresh, crusty bread. A pitcher of cool milk. A glistening pot of tea. All of it laid out invitingly on a crisp, spotless white tablecloth, edged in a diamond pattern of dull gold, under the warm luminescence of a hurricane lamp.

It looks good enough to eat, though it isn't: teapot and pitcher are empty, and the loaf, real as it seems, is a cleverly molded replica, complete even to the lumps and bumps that come from baking—and that makes the finished bread all the more appetizing!

One can almost smell the yeasty fragrance, imagine how the warm slices will taste, spread with fresh-churned butter and homemade jam or jelly—

> *But Anne could not eat. In vain she nibbled at the bread and butter and pecked at the crab-apple preserve out of the little*

As gleaming and bright as the fictional Marilla kept it, the hall at Green Gables offers glimpses of both Anne's and Maud's worlds, from the stiff postures of the Macneills to the little table where Marilla put Anne's hat that first night.

*scalloped glass dish by her plate. She did not really make any head-
way at all.*

*"You're not eating anything," said Marilla sharply, eyeing her
as if it were a serious shortcoming.*

Anne sighed.

*"I can't. I'm in the depths of despair. Can you eat when you're
in the depths of despair?"*

*"I've never been in the depths of despair, so I can't say,"
responded Marilla.*

"Weren't you? Well, did you try to imagine *you were in the depths
of despair?"*

I think of the orphaned child, knowing only the coldness and priva-
tion of institutional life or servitude to families with children of their
own. She is given new hope—a family wants to adopt her!—only to
have that hope dashed on the very portal of what she believes will be a
real home. Would I not be in the depths of despair, unable to eat despite
being famished after a long train journey?

Suddenly the "food" on the table looks like the imitation it is. Still
beautiful to behold, but the imagination's appetite has grown cold.

*"I guess she's tired," said Matthew, who hadn't spoken since his
return from the barn. "Best put her to bed, Marilla."*

*Marilla had been wondering where Anne should be put to bed.
She had prepared a couch in the kitchen chamber for the desired
and expected boy. But, although it was neat and clean, it did not
seem quite the thing to put a girl there somehow. But the spare
room was out of the question for such a stray waif, so there remained only the east gable room.*

A startlingly authentic-
looking replica of an evening
meal adorns the kitchen table
at Green Gables.

Anne's Room

"It isn't heavy," Anne tells Matthew on the journey from the Bright River station. "I've got all my worldly goods in it, but it isn't heavy."

Like the faded, small, and "extremely old" carpetbag, the tiny gable chamber to which Marilla escorts Anne that first unhappy night is as serviceable—and as unappealing—as its bare walls. As Anne's story unfolds, her unique personality transforms the room, just as our joys and sorrows are etched upon our faces in creases of laughter or in frown-lines.

But, being Anne, she does dream of new surroundings, and eventually the room is redecorated—in the novel by Marilla, in the "real" world by the historians and collectors who have helped make today's Green Gables such a faithful representation of the work and the era of Lucy Maud Montgomery.

So the room to which I ascend bears no resemblance to the one Anne views, wistfully, after Marilla takes her upstairs. The only physical record of the rigidity that "sent a shiver to the very marrow of Anne's bones" is the 6″ x 8″ mirror, the "prim yellow chair," and the carpetbag. For the rest, we must turn to the story.

> *The whitewashed walls were so painfully bare and staring that she thought they must ache over their own bareness. The floor was bare, too, except for a round braided mat in the middle....In one corner was the bed, a high, old-fashioned one, with four dark, low-turned posts. In the other corner was the ... three-cornered table adorned with a fat, red velvet pincushion hard enough to turn the point of the most adventurous pin. Above it hung a little six-by-eight mirror. Midway between table and bed was the window, with an icy white muslin frill over it, and opposite it was the wash-stand....With a sob she hastily discarded her garments, put on the skimpy nightgown and sprang into bed, where she burrowed face downward into the pillow and pulled the clothes over her head.*

I stand in the bright, cheery, refurbished room, and close my eyes, concentrating on that description until I can see it all, even to the slender form under the bedclothes. The child I see is almost completely still, but her shoulders are shaking—and I can hear muffled sobs.

It'll be better tomorrow, Anne, my mind whispers. *Even the room. You'll see.*

> *It was broad daylight when Anne awoke and sat up in bed staring confusedly at the window through which a flood of cheery sunshine was pouring and outside of which something white and feathery waved across glimpses of blue sky....yes, it was a cherry-tree in full bloom outside of her window.*

A Geranium Named Bonny

I wander down to the kitchen to explore more fully the room—or rooms, rather—where families of the era spent most of their time, especially on cold winter evenings, when they would gather around the wood stove to chat, read, sew, or knit.

Marilla and Matthew's stove is a good big one—a Waterloo #2, to be precise, built in Sackville, New Brunswick, in 1876. The peekaboo oven bulges over the cooking surface, under which the wood is burned. Like most stoves in nineteenth-century kitchens, it dominates the room, which seems strangely stark, almost sterile, for a place that is supposed to represent closeness, sharing, a feeling of family.

But then, Marilla and Matthew, although fundamentally good-hearted people, aren't given to strong displays of emotion; and Marilla, especially, emphasizes the practical, functional approach to life. A decent stove, boxes for wood and kindling, the necessities of cleaning—rug beater, feather duster, sock stretcher, and so on—along with chairs to sit on and a table to eat at. Of course, a well-stocked pantry with work-table for preparing food and washing dishes, and definitely the milk porch beyond—these, too, were essential. But no ruffles or frills.

Yet the longer I stay, the more this room's warmth begins to emerge, like sunlight poking through the oppressiveness of a cloudy day. It must be Anne, extending her observant, sensitive, affectionate presence to Marilla—along with an offer to do the breakfast dishes.

> *"What's to be done with you I don't know. Matthew is a most ridiculous man,"*
>
> *"I think he's lovely," said Anne reproachfully. "He is so very sympathetic. He didn't mind how much I talked—he seemed to like it. I felt that he was a kindred spirit as soon as ever I saw him."*
>
> *"You're both queer enough, if that's what you mean by kindred spirits," said Marilla with a sniff. "Yes, you may wash the dishes. Take plenty of hot water, and be sure you dry them well."*

I watch as light suffuses the room, lingering on the windowsill, transforming three humble geraniums into a scarlet blaze. Outside, the glory of summer abounds—flowers are everywhere, the fruit trees are lush with greens of every shade, and the air is so still and quiet and warm that through the open window I can hear bees buzzing, hovering hungrily over the wild roses. But the feeling of Anne's presence remains in the room, and mingled with the warmth of her all-but-palpable spirit I sense a sharp poignancy—and an almost desperate hope.

The battered and bruised carpetbag Anne takes with her to Green Gables, containing "all my worldly goods," is but one of the well-chosen antique pieces chosen to reflect the novel's interiors.

The big old Waterloo stove dominates the kitchen at Green Gables, as it would in any nineteenth-century farmhouse. The pantry is through the open door.

"I want to go out so much—everything seems to be calling to me, 'Anne, Anne, come out to us. Anne, Anne, we want a playmate'— but it's better not. There is no use in loving things if you have to be torn from them, is there? And it's so hard to keep from loving things, isn't it?"

Just so Lucy Maud Montgomery's anguished heart might have cried out, torn from her mother, shut up for so many years in what she felt was a loveless household; "resigned," as she says through Anne, "to my fate." Yet it is through Anne that Maud finds the way to live out her abundance of feeling. Her generous spirit gives Anne the depth of familial love that she, the author, was denied.

And it is the simple geranium plant that will mark the transition from a desperate hope to the certainty of belonging: the decision to keep Anne won't be made for some hours yet, but the intention is as clear as this glorious summer sky.

"But where on earth is the sense of naming a geranium?"

"Oh, I like things to have handles even if they are only geraniums. It makes them feel more like people. How do you know but that it hurts a geranium's feelings just to be called a geranium and nothing else? You wouldn't want to be called nothing but a woman all the time. Yes, I shall call it Bonny...."

"I never in all my life saw or heard anything to equal her," muttered Marilla, beating a hasty retreat down cellar after potatoes. "She is kind of interesting, as Matthew says. I can feel already that I'm wondering what on earth she'll say next. She'll be casting a spell over me, too...."

Not an "apple-scented geranium," like the one Anne notices on the kitchen windowsill—but these blazing red plants deserve names nevertheless. What might Anne call them?

Compassionate Vision

Just across the hall from the kitchen at Green Gables is the sitting-room—what we might call a dining-room, though the Victorian sitting-room also serves as a place to socialize over a cup of tea, or write letters on a summer's evening. Less formal than the parlour, but more elegant than the kitchen, the Green Gables sitting-room gets little use in winter, because its Empire Franklin stove is nowhere near as powerful as the old Waterloo—and probably because pragmatic Marilla can't see the sense of running two stoves at once (unless company's coming).

The rich wood of the table and sideboard, set off by the fresh, crisp white of the curtains and table linens, make the room an inviting place to Anne, who, still walking on air after just being told she *can* stay at Green Gables after all, is getting her first lesson in the difference between imagination and reality. Of course, Marilla—the teacher—doesn't yet know that she too has her work cut out for her. All she knows is that ten minutes have passed since she sent Anne to get an illustrated card from the mantelpiece in the sitting-room. On the card is the Lord's Prayer, which Marilla is determined that Anne will learn—lest she repeat the "extraordinary petition" of the night before, an improvised prayer ending with, of all things, " 'Yours respectfully, Anne Shirley'!"

Marilla laid down her knitting and marched after her with a grim expression. She found Anne standing motionless before a picture hanging on the wall between two windows, with her hands clasped behind her, her face uplifted, and her eyes astar with dreams....

"Anne, whatever are you thinking of?" demanded Marilla sharply.

Anne came back to earth with a start.

It's not the Lord's Prayer that Anne is looking at, but a "rather vivid chromo" titled "Christ Blessing Little Children." Unnoticed by either Marilla or Anne, who are, after all, in their own world, I try to get a closer look at the picture—a group of children crowded around the soulful figure of Jesus. One little girl in blue stands apart from the others; she seems very unhappy, and there's a sense of yearning about her, as if she is hoping to be noticed in her loneliness and alienation.

Compassion surges through me, and I glance to my side. I can almost see the red-haired child, still wearing the unbecoming yellowish-grey dress from the orphanage. The frock looks about two sizes too small, the fabric straining against her as she animatedly explains to Marilla why the picture has so captivated her.

"...I guess she hadn't any father or mother of her own. But she wanted to be blessed, too, so she just crept shyly up on the outside of the crowd, hoping nobody would notice her—except Him. I'm sure I know just how she felt. Her heart must have beat and her

The vivid imagery of the chromo, "Christ Blessing Little Children," provides an irresistible allure for the imaginative Anne, who promptly daydreamed herself into the scene—to Marilla's consternation.

hands must have got cold, like mine did when I asked you if I could stay. She was afraid He mightn't notice her. But it's likely He did, don't you think?

Marilla, true to her nature, wants no part of indulging such "irreverent" fancies in her young ward—especially the part about the artist giving Jesus a sad countenance that couldn't possibly have appealed so strongly to the children flocking around him. All she wants is for Anne to learn some healthy, practical, morally appropriate habits, like memorizing the "Our Father" for her bedtime prayers. (Anne, in fact, will shortly refer to the words as "beautiful" and learn them with startling speed, a retentive ability not unlike that of her creator.)

Yet there is a gentleness that softens Marilla's tall, angular figure and relaxes the prim-and-proper demeanour as she leads Anne out of the sitting-room and back to the kitchen to start learning the prayer by heart. It seems she understands, deep down, why this little orphan, whose childhood has been a sad tale of loss, hardship, toil in other people's homes, would be drawn to the child in the picture.

Her Room of Dreams

The prayer is committed to memory before Anne even gets up the stairs to the east gable, where she sits by the window of her tiny, spare, and decidedly unromantic room. Time for some renovations, she decides—

"The walls, hung not with gold and silver brocade tapestry, but with a dainty apple-blossom paper, were adorned with a few good pictures...." This is Anne's "dainty nest."

"The floor is covered with a white velvet carpet with pink roses all over it and there are pink silk curtains at the windows. The walls are hung with gold and silver brocade tapestry. The furniture is mahogany. I never saw any mahogany, but it does sound so luxurious. This is a couch all heaped with gorgeous silken cushions, pink and blue and crimson and gold, and I am reclining gracefully on it. I can see my reflection in that splendid big mirror hanging on the wall...."

But by the time Anne reaches the little mirror and studies her own reflection, she has realized that she will not see "the Lady Cordelia Fitzgerald," all ivory skin and raven tresses, bedecked in lace and pearls. And that's all right, too; " 'It's a million times nicer to be Anne of Green Gables than Anne of nowhere in particular, isn't it?' "

Yes, it certainly is, I answer silently. I'd like to tell her that she'll have her pink silk curtains and mahogany furniture someday, but it wouldn't be true. And she wouldn't hear me, anyway. Still, there's a middle ground between Anne's wild imagination and Marilla's ascetic practicality—a place where the two extremes work wonders on each other instead of clashing. This is the room Anne will have—though she doesn't have the slightest inkling of it yet—"as sweet and dainty a nest as a young girl could desire."

The floor was covered with a pretty matting, and the curtains that softened the high windows and fluttered in the fragrant breezes were of pale green art muslin. The walls, hung not with gold and silver brocade tapestry but with a dainty apple-blossom paper, were adorned with a few good pictures....There was no "mahogany furniture," but there was a white-painted bookcase filled with books, a cushioned wicker rocker, a toilet-table befrilled with white muslin, a quaint, gilt-framed mirror with chubby pink cupids and purple grapes painted over its arched top, that used to hang in the spare room, and a low white bed.

All this is years away: Anne and Marilla's relationship will have to undergo many trials before everything starts coming up roses (not to mention pink cupids and purple grapes!). And the trouble starts almost immediately. First, there's the run-in with Marilla's nosy but essentially good-hearted neighbour, Mrs. Rachel Lynde—whose "skinny and homely" description of Anne earns the angry child's retort that Mrs. Lynde is "fat and clumsy." No sooner have the two of them made amends than there's the matter of the new dresses, which are plain, practical, and "not—pretty," as Anne puts it, deeply offending the well-intentioned Marilla, who is further dismayed to hear that Anne has unaccountably pinned buttercups and pink roses to her hat, perched over red braids and the new black-and-white sateen frock, on the occasion of her first expedition to Sunday school.

But the worst is yet to come. I shudder as I make my way to Marilla's room, thinking of the brooch....

A few feminine touches relieve the heavy, dark furniture in Marilla's room at Green Gables—lacy curtains, cheery wallpaper and, of course, the famous amethyst brooch, on the nightstand where it belongs!

The Amethyst Brooch

It's a dignified room—but I wouldn't want to live in it. Too dark, too oppressive. Even in broad daylight, the lit lamp provides welcome illumination. Yet this room neither frightens nor repels a visitor. A few softening touches relieve the gloom—lacy curtains, blue-flowered wallpaper, a black lace shawl draped over the dark-red chenille bedspread, and, over on the nightstand, a lace scarf, an old photo, and—yes, Marilla's most-prized possession. The amethyst brooch.

What a romantic story, I reflect, gazing at the violet gleam of the beautiful stone within the oval-shaped brooch. Given to Marilla's mother by an uncle who went to sea, then handed down to Marilla, it contains a tiny braid of her mother's hair. You really *can't* judge by appearances: who would have thought that a woman as down-to-earth, and, well, almost hard-edged, would have a sentimental streak?

But then, characters in books are just as complicated as "real" people. Maud's grandmother, Mrs. Macneill, was every bit as tough-minded and practical—and rigid—as Marilla. If not more. Yet who's to say that Mrs. Macneill didn't have an amethyst brooch hidden away somewhere?

My eyes fixed on the purple light reflecting from the gemstone, I suddenly remember an odd "coincidence" concerning amethysts. Maud's wedding present from her husband-to-be, Reverend Ewan Macdonald, was a necklace of amethysts and pearls.

No wonder Marilla is so devastated—and angry—when the brooch goes missing and she thinks Anne has lost, or taken, something as precious as the keepsake from her mother. " 'And how wicked of the child to deny having taken it, when anybody could see she must have. With such an innocent face, too!' " The longer Marilla holds on to her certainty that all is exactly as it appears—Anne has admitted to trying on the brooch; she is the last person to have handled it; therefore she has taken it and is lying about having returned it—the more complicated events become, until the very fabric of trust between them threatens to split down the middle.

Desperate to attend a Sunday-school picnic with her new friend, Diana Barry (on whose property is located the Lake of Shining Waters), Anne spins a yarn she hopes will placate Marilla, who doesn't believe the truth and insists upon a confession. The brooch, Anne says, is at the bottom of the "lake" after having slipped through her fingers while she was holding it up to catch the sunlight. This story only makes matters worse—not only is there to be no picnic for Anne, but Marilla dubs her " 'the very wickedest girl I ever heard of.' "

Talk about tangled webs! How can there possibly be a way out of this one?

> *When her dishes were washed and her bread sponge set and her hens fed Marilla remembered that she had noticed a small rent in her best black lace shawl when she had taken it off on Monday afternoon on returning from the Ladies' Aid. She would go and mend it.*
>
> *The shawl was in a box in her trunk. As Marilla lifted it out, the sunlight, falling through the vines that clustered thickly about the window, struck upon something caught in the shawl—something that glittered and sparkled in facets of violet light. Marilla snatched at it with a gasp.*
>
> *It was the amethyst brooch, hanging by a thread of the lace by its catch!*

In an instant, sunlight ends the nightmare. Significantly, Marilla is equally quick to apologize. And there's even time for Anne to be whisked away to the picnic ground in plenty of time for tea with Diana and the other children.

Down Lovers' Lane

"I was happy—content—at peace," Lucy Maud Montgomery writes in her journals. "I was neither young nor old—I was ageless. The past and the present were one and there was no future. I moved in an enchanted circle beyond which there was no time, within which there was no change."

Just below Green Gables curves a wide path lined with tall, stately trees stretching their branches to catch the sun. Patches of light filter through the leaves, embroidering lacy patterns upon the forest floor. Maud's enchanting words echo in my ears, erasing the decades between us—what can linear time mean in a place like this?

Lovers' Lane: Anne's name for the pathway she and Diana Barry take to and from school, starting just below the orchard at Green Gables and extending into the woods to the edge of the Cuthbert farm. The road has another purpose—a secondary one, as far as the girls are concerned—which is as a way to get the cows to and from pasture, and wood for the stoves hauled home in winter. I follow their route as if I knew it by heart, as if Maud were guiding me "up the lane under the leafy arch of maples...."

Lovers' Lane leads into the beautifully overgrown, leafy enclosure of Balsam Hollow, with its tall, stately trees illuminated by a diffusion of light.

A "leafy arch" of trees leads down the pathway that Maud loved to travel, and that Anne also claimed as sanctuary (or delightful route to school with Diana). They all called it Lovers' Lane.

Lovers' Lane, the old log bridge, and the babbling brook—these are really Maud's places explored—and named—years before she ever contemplated writing *Anne of Green Gables*. In this enchanted realm, where everything is possible, I, like Maud, believe in a real Anne, braids flying in the breeze, pursued by plump little dark-haired Diana, the two of them hurtling down the Birch Path, "where the light came down sifted through so many emerald screens that it was as flawless as the heart of a diamond."

It was fringed in all its length with slim young birches, white-stemmed and lissom-boughed; ferns and starflowers and wild lilies-of-the-valley and scarlet tufts of pigeon berries grew along it; and always there was a delightful spiciness in the air and music of bird calls and the murmur and laugh of wood winds overhead.

I look around at the kaleidoscope of colours glimmering through the woods. Some people say there are more shades of green here than in Ireland, and I can see why. The brilliant emeralds, cool jades, the greens tinged with ochre or brown, the clear grass-greens, translucent as glass, the silvers and blacks and blues that mingle with evergreen—

On the Birch Path, the light does indeed flow through "emerald screens," dazzling yet soft as the forest floor beneath.

Suddenly I see a shadow beside a birch. Or is it two shadows? The faintest sound of laughter ripples through the woods. The very air seems charged with anticipation. But just as quickly it is over, and I am alone with Maud's words about Anne, so clearly can I hear them.

Anne is so real that, although I've never met her, I feel quite sure I shall do so someday, perhaps in a stroll through Lovers' Lane in the twilight, or in the moonlit Birch Path. I shall lift my eyes and find her, child or maiden, by my side. And I shall not be in the least surprised, because I have always known she was somewhere.

Just then, shadow becomes substance, and a small, slender girl dashes past me up the Birch Path. Her braids are unmistakably red. Bright red.

About Boys and Slates

Back at Green Gables, I race up the steep staircase, almost colliding with two startled visitors on their way downstairs after completing their tour. "Sorry!" I gasp. "I just needed to check something." They nod, smiling doubtfully.

I look into Anne's room. Empty. Did I really think she'd be there?

The afternoon light creates dancing shadows across the bright little room, and my eyes follow them over to a dark wooden chest next to the dressing-table. Inside the chest are all Anne's little mementos and on top are a bird's nest and two school slates. I smile at the sight of these objects, so rich in their associations with Anne's story. The nest, handiwork of an industrious blue jay, is no doubt Anne's spoils from a nature outing organized for the Avonlea students by her beloved teacher Miss Stacy. As for the slates—especially the one that's broken—therein lies another tale.

I suppose we've all had a Gilbert Blythe in our lives—someone we love to hate, hate to love; someone with whom we compete violently, for fear we will reveal our true feelings of affection. Or someone we ignore—with a passion.

Certainly Lucy Maud Montgomery had a Gilbert Blythe in *her* life, which is probably why she renamed him and set him smack dab in the middle of Anne's world. His real name was Nate Lockhart, a classmate of Maud's at Cavendish school whose obvious devotion in no way dampered her fierce competitiveness with him for marks and prizes. And although they did have a romantic relationship, for a time, it was clearly a stormy one, as this excerpt from a December 1890 letter to her friend Penzie Macneill attests: "I think you are too awfully mean for anything to keep teasing me eternally about that detestable pig Nate Lockhart. You know I hate him and if you ever mention his name in your letters again I'll never write to you again. So there."

Ah, true love! Eventually those cruel words were forgotten and the two did become friends again; and at least Maud never broke a slate over Nate's head—not that I know of, anyway—as she had Anne do to Gilbert at school one fateful day. Of course, if Nate had offered Maud this sort of provocation, perhaps she would have been as disinclined to resist her tempestuous impulses as Anne was:

Gilbert Blythe wasn't used to putting himself out to make a girl look at him and meeting with failure. She should look at him, that red-haired Shirley girl with the little pointed chin and the big eyes that weren't like the eyes of any other girl in Avonlea school.

Gilbert reached across the aisle, picked up the end of Anne's long red braid, held it out at arm's length and said in a piercing whisper:

"Carrots! Carrots!"

Then Anne looked at him with a vengeance!

She did more than look. She sprang to her feet, her bright fancies fallen into careless ruin. She flashed one indignant glance at Gilbert from eyes whose angry sparkle was swiftly quenched in equally angry tears.

"You mean, hateful boy!" she exclaimed passionately. "How dare you?"

And then—Thwack! Anne had brought her slate down on Gilbert's head and cracked it—slate, not head—clear across.

Punished by the unpleasant and unsympathetic Mr. Phillips for her display of "such a temper and such a vindictive spirit," Anne is forced to stand in front of the class all afternoon. Such is her feeling of anguish and humiliation that, despite Gilbert's attempt to intercede on her behalf, his after-school apology, and his subsequent efforts to make friends, Anne holds firm to her resolve never to forgive him. At least for a good many years.

Not to mention Mr. Phillips, who not only wrote on the blackboard above her head that she had a bad temper, but spelled her name without the treasured "e." *Twice.*

School life, unpleasant and pleasant. This broken slate looks suspiciously like the one Anne broke over Gilbert's head when he teased her about having red hair. The nest is a blue jay's, a relic from one of Anne's nature outings—or one very much like it.

The Raspberry Cordial

> Raspberry Cordial
> Real raspberry cordial is prepared by mashing 4 quarts of ripe raspberries in a stone jar with 1 pound of white sugar. Pour over them 1 quart of the best cider vinegar, and set the jar in the hot sunshine for 4 hours, after which the mixture is strained, bottled, and sealed. Lay the bottles in a cool cellar. For drinking, stir 2 tablespoons of the mixture into a tumbler of iced water.
>
> (Courtesy of Green Gables House, Prince Edward Island National Park.)

As much as she hated Gilbert, however, did she love Diana, with all the love of her passionate little heart, equally intense in its likes and dislikes.

Cordial. The *Collins English Dictionary* defines it as a drink with a fruit base, and the Victorians made it by mixing ripe fruit, sugar, and cider vinegar, slightly fermenting the concoction before serving a small amount of it in a large glass of water. Effervescent and pleasant—like the other meaning of the word *cordial*. But the mild fermentation doesn't make this beverage intoxicating, which is why Marilla suggests Anne share some with Diana for their first tea together at Green Gables.

Already delighted at the prospect of cherry preserves, fruit-cake, and cookies; already imagining herself at the head of the sitting-room table, pouring out tea (although, alas, not from the pot that belongs to the precious rosebud-spray tea set!), Anne erupts with sheer delight at the mention of the raspberry cordial—left over from a recent church social. She flies over to her beloved friend's house to tell her the good news, and the two are soon cosily situated at the table, telling tales of school life and relating the trials of cookery—how forgetting the flour *does* tend to ruin a cake, and how it is probably best to refrain from revealing to stylish guests that a dead mouse has recently been discovered in a dish of plum-pudding sauce.

Through all this Diana is thoroughly enjoying the raspberry cordial. " 'The nicest I ever drank,' " she says. Trouble is, the "bright red hue" of the drink has its origin in currants, not raspberries; Diana is guzzling Marilla's currant wine, not cordial. And for once Anne is entirely blameless; Marilla has stored the cordial down in the cellar, forgotten all about it, and told Anne to take the bottle that is in the sitting-room pantry. The bottle that deals a death-blow to Anne's friendship with her number-one kindred spirit, who staggers home, completely intoxicated to her outraged family.

In vain Marilla tries to intercede with the infuriated Mrs. Barry, who forbids Diana from ever playing with Anne again, and who tells the "culprit," when she comes to plead for mercy: " 'I don't think you are a fit little girl for Diana to associate with.' "

The children are allowed to bid each other good-bye, but, as Anne puts it, " 'Ten minutes isn't very long to say an eternal farewell in.' " Still, they do their best.

It's back in the kitchen hutch *now,* but Marilla did make a mistake about the bottle of raspberry cordial she intended for Anne and Diana's tea. And the girls got into the currant wine instead!

> *"In the years to come thy memory will shine like a star over my lonely life, as that last story we read together says. Diana, wilt thou give me a lock of thy jet-black tresses in parting to treasure for evermore?"*
>
> *"Have you got anything to cut it with?" queried Diana, wiping away the tears which Anne's affecting accents had caused to flow afresh, and returning to practicalities.*
>
> *"Yes. I've got my patchwork scissors in my apron pocket, fortunately," said Anne. She solemnly clipped one of Diana's curls. "Fare thee well, my beloved friend. Henceforth we must be as strangers though living side by side. But my heart will ever be faithful to thee."*

A Friend in Need

Poor Anne! And it isn't even her fault! I glance up at the kitchen hutch, filled with every manner of bowl, crock, jar, and bottle—including the corked container of cordial, which Marilla has brought back up from the cellar to store in the hutch. The bright-red liquid almost reaches the top of the bottle; it doesn't seem anyone has had much of a thirst for raspberry cordial recently.

What could possibly set things right between Anne and Diana again, I wonder; reflecting.

An image bursts into my mind, as clear as the glass that contains the ruby drink. There is Matthew, comfortably seated in his rocking chair, and Anne, sitting at the kitchen table chatting about geometry and Mr. Phillips, who apparently considers the child much improved after the broken-slate incident. Marilla is in Charlottetown with Mrs. Lynde and just about everyone else from Avonlea and surroundings, to hear a speech by the Premier (we'd use the title Prime Minister today), and won't return until next morning. Meanwhile, Anne is about to get herself and Matthew a plate of russets to help her get through her lessons, and, presumably, aid Matthew in the digestion of his *Farmers' Advocate*.

All things great are wound up with all things little. At first glance it might not seem that the decision of a certain Canadian Premier to include Prince Edward Island in a political tour could have anything to do with the fortunes of little Anne Shirley at Green Gables. But it had.

I turn from the kitchen hutch to view the pantry, an important extension of the kitchen, where Anne did the dishes and helped Marilla prepare the meals. This is where left-over foods are stored, such as the plum pudding Anne forgot to cover. Above the work-table are shelves—ingredients for cooking and baking, cookbooks, medicines. *Ipecac*. What an odd-sounding word, isn't it? That's the name of a root whose extract is used to make emetics, those nasty-tasting potions used to induce vomiting, or as an expectorant...

Just left of the pantry is the milk porch, where the cellar door is located. Here is where Marilla discovered the dish, apples, and extinguished candle at the bottom of the cellar steps. It seems that Anne was startled when Diana barged into the kitchen, terribly upset; her baby sister was desperately ill with the croup, and the hired girl, Young Mary Joe, had no idea what to do. But Matthew and Anne did—one headed out to find a doctor, and the other, reunited with her friend if only for the moment, goes to the rescue. Being in service was an emotional ordeal for the sensitive Anne, but it taught her the skills she now needs; for " 'Mrs Hammond had twins three times,' " and they all had croup regularly.

Desperate to help her friend's sister, Anne grabs a bottle of ipecac from the shelves above the work table in the pantry. Off the milk porch are the cellar stairs where her candle and plate of apples went tumbling at the sound of Diana's precipitous arrival.

But before the two girls leave, Anne needs something. I glance again at the pantry shelf .... Of course, the bottle of ipecac!

It was three o'clock when Matthew came with the doctor, for he had been obliged to go all the way to Spencervale for one. But the pressing need for assistance was past. Minnie May was much better and was sleeping soundly.

"I was awfully near giving up in despair," explained Anne. "She got worse and worse until she was sicker than ever the Hammond twins were, even the last pair. I gave her every drop of ipecac in that bottle, and when the last dose went down, I said to

myself, 'This is the last lingering hope and I fear 'tis a vain one.' But in about three minutes she coughed up the phlegm and began to get better right away. You must just imagine my relief, doctor, because I can't express it in words."

He looked at Anne as if he were thinking some things about her that couldn't be expressed in words. Later on, however, he expressed them to Mr and Mrs Barry.

"That little red-headed girl they have over at Cuthbert's is as smart as they make 'em. I tell you she saved that baby's life, for it would have been too late by the time I got here."

The bright pastel shades and gleaming white furniture make the spare room a most inviting place for Anne—all the more inviting because it is kept *only* for visitors.

Before the frosty winter morning is over, Mrs. Barry is at Green Gables to deliver the news that, at this point, may not altogether shock the reader: Diana and Anne can be friends again, and Mrs. Barry is properly penitent for her harsh words towards Anne.

But what if Mrs. Hammond hadn't had three pairs of twins? What if the Premier hadn't been speaking in Charlottetown, and the doctor had gotten there earlier?

The Spare Room

Closer than ever, the two girls spend a wonderful afternoon together at the Barrys', complete with tea from the very best china set, as if Anne were "real company." Thus reinstalled in her kindred spirit's life, Anne gets the signal one evening from Diana that special plans are brewing; this elaborate communication system is explained briefly by its inventor:

"We set the candle on the window-sill and make flashes by passing the cardboard back and forth....Two flashes mean, 'Are you there?' Three mean 'yes' and four 'no.' Five mean, 'Come over as soon as possible, because I have something to reveal'."

The revelation, in this case, is that Anne has been invited to stay the night at Diana's—*maybe even in the spare room*—after voyaging to the school's Debating Club concert in a big sleigh driven by Diana's cousins from Newbridge.

And all this in honour of Diana's birthday, a desperate Anne pleads with Marilla, who is refusing to let her go; and " 'it isn't as if birthdays were common things, Marilla." But this approach works no better than Anne's bid for the honour of sleeping in the Barrys' spare-room bed. (A spare room, always furnished with the very best and reserved for special guests, is kept ready in every home in Avonlea—or Cavendish, for that matter.)

No, Marilla remains as stubborn as—well, perhaps Maud's grandparents, who forbade her from attending or participating in the twice-yearly concerts at Cavendish Hall. Perhaps they, like Marilla, believed such outings would make a girl " 'vain and forward and fond of gadding.' " Adds Marilla, annoyed by Matthew after a tearful Anne has gone to bed: " 'She'd go there and catch cold like as not, and have her head filled up with nonsense and excitement. It would unsettle her for a week. I understand that child's disposition and what's good for it better than you do, Matthew.' "

I leave the kitchen and walk slowly upstairs.

The door to the spare room stands ajar, a lamp illuminating its cheerful interior; the spool bed, with its tulip-embossed quilt and plump white pillows against the intricately carved headboard, looks especially inviting. *I wonder if the Barrys' spare room is so pretty, and oh, I hope Anne has the chance to find out!* After all, Maud's teacher Miss Gordon persuaded the Macneills to allow Maud to attend school concerts, so...

> *The next morning, when Anne was washing the breakfast dishes in the pantry, Matthew paused on his way out to the barn to say to Marilla again:*
>
> *"I think you ought to let Anne go, Marilla."*
>
> *For a moment Marilla looked things not lawful to be uttered. Then she yielded to the inevitable and said tartly:*
>
> *"Very well, she can go, since nothing else'll please you."*

We all need a moderating influence on our conviction that our rules are ideal, unassailable. It's true that Marilla *is* able to say "I told you so," for Matthew's benefit, when she hears that the two girls have utterly discomfited Diana's elderly maiden aunt, Miss Josephine Barry, by leaping onto the bed in the Barrys' spare room in the mistaken belief that the chamber was unoccupied. But Anne has set things right in a conversation with Miss Barry—who had been ready to leave the house and refuse to pay for Diana's music-lessons after all. And it is Anne (appropriately enough) who has the last word on the matter:

> *"Miss Barry was a kindred spirit, after all," Anne confided to Marilla. "You wouldn't think so to look at her, but she is. You don't find it out right at first, as in Matthew's case, but after awhile you come to see it. Kindred spirits are not so scarce as I used to think. It's splendid to find out there are so many of them in the world."*

The Haunted Wood

As I leave the Green Gables framhouse to take a look at Anne's Haunted Wood, across from the front of the farm, I am so certain I will not be afraid that I wait until dusk to head over. After all, I know that Anne and Diana made up all that stuff about skeletons and headless men, just to amuse themselves. And if that weren't enough, I also happen to know the name Haunted Wood came straight from the author herself; she played there as a child with her mates, Well and Dave.

> *"The Haunted Wood was a harmless, pretty spruce grove in the field below the orchard, recalls Maud in "The Alpine Path." We considered that all our haunts were too commonplace, so we invented this for our amusement. None of us really believed at first that the grove was haunted, or the mysterious "white things" which we pretended to see flitting through it at dismal hours were aught but the creations of our own fancy. But our minds were weak and our imaginations strong; we soon came to believe implicitly in our myths, and not one of us could have gone near that grove after sunset on pain of death. Death! What was death compared to the unearthly possibility of falling into the clutches of a "White thing?"*

That isn't going to happen to *me*. Yet as I reach the edge of the small grove of swaying spruce, an odd feeling comes over me. The gloom of the woods suddenly looks ominous, and Anne's words to Marilla—who has asked her to run over to Diana's on an errand—return to me on the moaning wind.

> *"Oh, Marilla, I wouldn't go through the Haunted Wood after dark now for anything. I'd be sure that white things would reach out from behind the trees and grab me."*
>
> *"Anne Shirley, do you mean to tell me you believe all that wicked nonsense of your own imagination?"*
>
> *"Not believe* exactly,*" faltered Anne. "At least, I don't believe it in daylight. But after dark, Marilla, it's different. That is when ghosts walk."*
>
> *"There are no such things as ghosts, Anne."*

Bravely I push on into the wood. But the haunting vibration of the wind through the dead and decaying trees is impossible to ignore. I look up at the stripped trunks, the white branches, like the skeletal arms of—ghosts! On and on I walk—it seems like the longest distance I've ever walked in my life, convinced that every ghost and ghoul of my childhood fairy tales is lurking behind a tree, waiting for me. How I sympathize with poor Anne, forced by Marilla to finally take that dreaded route at night, " 'just for a lesson and a warning.' "

Bitterly did she repent the licence she had given to her imagination. The goblins of her fancy lurked in every shadow about her, reaching out their cold, fleshless hands to grasp the terrified small girl who had called them into being....The swoop of bats in the darkness over her was as the wings of unearthly creatures. When she reached Mr William Bell's field she fled across it as if pursued by an army of white things....

Somehow I get through the wood without breaking into a run. Somehow I face the "dreadful return journey," and this without closing my eyes on the way back, as Anne did. And somehow I make my way back to the safety of the old farmhouse.

Watch out for "white things" if you venture into this spruce grove near Green Gables after dark. That is, if you believe in that sort of "nonsense," as Marilla might put it.

An Unforgettable Cake

Safely back at Green Gables, I take refuge in the first room I see—which happens to be the elegant, beautifully furnished, and altogether formidable parlour. Unlike the cheerful sitting-room, this formal and foreboding apartment conjures up thoughts of ironclad rules of etiquette, black-clad dignitaries sitting stiffly on the sofa, and the chilling image of a rosewood casket; the Victorians often displayed their dead in the parlour. Thankfully, there is no such replication attempted here, but all the other furnishings are typical of the era—the horsehair furniture, lace curtains, rose-and-fern-patterned carpet, and knick-knack shelf, which was called a whatnot.

This is a formal place, designed for ritual—not a place to relax, and certainly not the kind of place I want to be after my ordeal in the Haunted Wood. I'm about to leave when, like a memory awakened, I hear the sound of clinking teacups—and exclamations of delight. Turning around, I recognize Marilla, Matthew, and Anne—but who is the young couple sitting with them? Looking over the tea-table for clues, I'm greeted by a magnificent feast for the eye. Masses of pink roses and delicate ferns swirl gracefully around plate after plate of delicacies: cold jellied chicken and tongue, lemon and cherry pie, three different kinds of cookies, baking-powder biscuits, fruit-cake, preserves, and a lovely, fluffy layer cake filled with ruby-red jelly. And there in the centre is the rosebud tea set—it must be the minister and his wife come to tea.

Yes, that's right— Mr. and Mrs. Allan. I remember. And they're having such a splendid time! Too bad there's a disaster in the offing....And Anne has done so well, it seems—charming the Allans with her floral arrangement, even baking that fabulous-looking cake. It can't be raspberry cordial this time, so what could go wrong?

The cake? Oh, no, not the beautiful layer cake...

> *"Mercy on us, Anne, you've flavoured the cake with anodyne liniment. I broke the liniment bottle last week and poured what was left into an old empty vanilla bottle. I suppose it's partly my fault— I should have warned you—but for pity's sake why couldn't you have smelled it?"*
>
> *Anne dissolved into tears under this double disgrace.*
>
> *"I couldn't—I had such a cold!" and with this she fairly fled to the gable chamber, where she cast herself on the bed and wept as one who refuses to be comforted.*

Of course she *is* comforted—not by Marilla's curt but loving tones, this time, but by Mrs. Allan, who comes up to her room to assure her it's a mistake anyone could make. Not only does she recognize that Anne's hopes for the cake are more important than the outcome, she also knows enough to ask for a tour of the child's flower garden, allowing her to display an accomplishment after all.

Puffed Sleeves

They did not see Matthew, who shrank bashfully back into the shadows beyond the wood-box....Anne stood among them, bright-eyed and animated as they; but Matthew became conscious that there was something about her different from her mates....

He had recourse to his pipe that evening to help him study it out, much to Marilla's disgust. After two hours of smoking and hard reflection Matthew arrived at the solution of his problem. Anne was not dressed like the other girls.

Like Anne, Maud was not dressed like the other girls. If the Macneills were particular about the books their granddaughter read, the few friends she was allowed to visit, and the social outings she was permitted to attend, they were equally unbending about what she wore. "Baby aprons" and high button shoes were the rule when it came to school clothes, as Maud recalls in "The Alpine Path," while the other girls wore pinafores and were allowed to go shoeless in warm weather. But the biggest blow came when Maud begged her grandparents to let her have bangs cut in her hair—the very latest fashion statement among the young ladies of Cavendish. Nothing could persuade them; and Maud never forgot the incident.

Marilla kept her clothed in plain, dark dresses, all made after the same unvarying pattern. If Matthew knew there was such a thing as fashion in dress it is as much as he did; but he was quite sure that Anne's sleeves did not look at all like the sleeves the other girls wore. He recalled the cluster of little girls he had seen around her that evening—all gay in waists of red and blue and pink and white—and he wondered why Marilla always kept her so plainly and soberly gowned.

But unlike Maud, who did not have the opportunity to be the author of her own childhood, Anne is the beneficiary of all the understanding and love her creator felt was denied her. More than once, Matthew sees to it that Anne is allowed to blossom, to spread her wings and fly the coop Marilla has built—as he does when he insists she attend Diana's birthday celebration. As he does when he sits in his corner, smoking and thinking about her clothing dilemma.

Surely it would do no harm to let the child have one pretty dress—something like Diana Barry always wore. Matthew decided that he would give her one....Christmas was only a fortnight off.

Nor does Marilla fall into the role of black-hat villain. She yields to Matthew when it's clear that he's right, and her sniffs of weary resignation are mostly show, a thin veil over the very real appreciation she has of Anne's essence—which her apparently harsh rules seek only to

Like a latter-day living room, only much more formal, the Victorian parlour at Green Gables features horsehair furniture and a whatnot (a knick-knack shelf).

Marilla's rosebud-spray tea set has somehow found its way into the sitting-room, although it would normally reside in the more formal parlour.

Opposite page:

Beyond the kitchen wood-box at Green Gables is a rocking chair in a little corner favoured by Marilla's brother, Matthew. Here he would smoke his pipe (much to Marilla's disgust) and browse through the *Farmers' Advocate*.

It took Matthew a couple of hours with his pipe to come up with a solution to his dilemma about Anne. He would get her a dress for Christmas—with Mrs. Rachel's help, that is.

One of "snuffy-coloured gingham," one of "an ugly blue shade"—both made by Marilla for Anne, whose reaction was as plain as the dresses: " 'I'll imagine that I like them'."

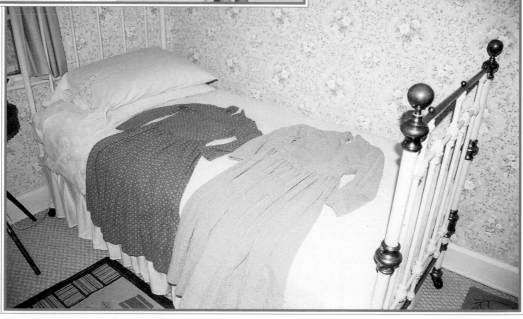

protect, not repress. So too, perhaps, were Maud's grandparents, though sadly without enough of the ability to yield that Marilla displayed when, on Christmas morning, she "feigned to be contemptuously filling the teapot, but nevertheless watched the scene out of the corner of her eye with a rather interested air."

> *Anne took the dress and looked at it in reverent silence. Oh, how pretty it was—a lovely soft brown gloria with all the gloss of silk; a skirt with dainty frills and shirrings; a waist elaborately pin-tucked in the most fashionable way, with a little ruffle of filmy lace at the neck. But the sleeves—they were the crowning glory. Long elbow cuffs and above them two beautiful puffs divided by rows of shirring and bows of brown silk ribbon.*
>
> *"That's a Christmas present for you, Anne," said Matthew shyly. "Why—why—Anne, don't you like it? Well now—well now."*
>
> *For Anne's eyes had suddenly filled with tears.*

The brook in Balsam Hollow really *does* babble as it winds its way through nests of buttercups and ferns.

The Way Things Change

Recitations make her the "bright particular star" of the school Christmas concert; school becomes an exciting place when Miss Stacy arrives, bringing such delights (for Anne, anyway) as compositions on "A Winter's Walk in the Woods"; and Anne makes the rite of passage from girlhood to young womanhood, turning thirteen in the spring. A new coat, navy blue broadcloth, made by a real dressmaker over at Carmody; a trip to Charlottetown with Diana to visit Miss Barry for *four days,* and even the "elegant" spare room to sleep in. Yes, Anne is all grown up now; we know this for certain when she tells Marilla, after the trip to Miss Barry's, that the honour of spending the night in the spare room " 'isn't what I used to think it was.

'The things you wanted so much when you were a child don't seem half so wonderful to you when you get them.' "

Rather a sad thought—Anne without desperate desires, Anne too sophisticated for the thrill of sleeping in the spare room, Anne who never gets into scrapes any more. But we needn't worry just yet, especially about the last bit. The spring Anne turns thirteen, she dyes her hair green, believing a pedlar who tells her it will be jet black.

No sooner have her shorn locks grown out to their usual colour (diplomatic Diana insists the shade is now closer to auburn than red), Anne almost drowns in the Lake of Shining Waters while the girls are attempting to re-enact a portion of the Arthurian legend. Further clouding any image of herself as a proper young lady, she spurns yet another offer of friendship from her rescuer, Gilbert Blythe, who happens by in Herman Andrew's dory just as Anne, who is playing the love-stricken corpse of Elaine drifting down to Camelot in a black-draped barge (Mr. Barry's flat), abandons her sinking vessel and clings for dear life to a bridge pile.

Still dreaming of raven locks, still all too ready for adventure, still fierce in her likes and dislikes (after all, Gilbert has been trying for two years to make amends for his "Carrots" remark about her hair). And still determined to make "a great improvement," as she assures Matthew and Marilla.

> But Matthew, who had been sitting mutely in his corner, laid a hand on Anne's shoulder when Marilla had gone out.
> "Don't give up all your romance, Anne," he whispered shyly, "a little of it is a good thing—not too much, of course—but keep a little of it, Anne, keep a little of it."

I wander out of the house and down Lovers' Lane, towards Balsam Hollow and the brook, which *does* babble as it wends its way through thick bushes and fairylike ferns, dotted with glistening buttercups. Shafts of light, diffused by all that intensity of green, transport me into a dream world, where my senses are filled with colour and shadow, birdsong and gentle breezes, the scent of pine and the warmth of summer sunlight.

When I'm ready to leave, twilight is falling, and the long shadows darken the path before me. *How quickly everything changes!*

But some things don't. A few things. Look at Anne, all grown up but still the same dedicated romantic—all excited after her sojourn in the big city but yearning for her little room in the east gable, " 'knowing even in my sleep that the stars were shining outside and that the wind was blowing in the firs across the brook.' " I peer into the kitchen, where Anne, I recall, having arrived back from Charlottetown, would be chatting to Marilla and Matthew about the trip.

"I've had a splendid time," she concluded happily, "and I feel that it marks an epoch in my life. But the best of it all was the coming home."

Remembering Matthew

It's a tiny room off the hall between the sitting-room and the kitchen. A typical man's room, with checked coverlet over a three-quarter-size bed; simple furniture, plain wallpaper, muslin curtains at the high window. Rather a bright room, for all that it's downstairs—Matthew's heart condition stopped him from climbing the steep stairway two years before Anne arrived at Green Gables—and, despite its small size (or maybe because of it), quite an appealing place.

No-one is here, but that's not surprising. Bedrooms of the era were for sleeping, not daydreaming an afternoon away. Probably Matthew is out in the orchard, or in the hayfield below the barn, or in his rocker by the wood-box.

I look everywhere for some sign of the gaunt, frowsy-headed, ageing but ageless man who has never failed to make me smile whenever I see and hear him on this journey through Anne's world. But he is nowhere to be found. Maybe I just haven't looked in all the right places, or could be I've missed him; when you're as quiet and shy as Matthew, people often overlook you. They don't mean to, but they do.

Not Marilla, though. She might sigh with exasperation when her brother becomes obstinate over an issue like Anne staying at Green Gables, but she doesn't ignore Matthew—and she's always glad of it later. As for Anne, if there's anyone who could take the place of the father she never knew, that someone is Matthew, glorying in Anne's success at the teaching college, Queen's, and her scholarship to Redmond College; insisting, in his gentle way, that "his girl" needs a new dress (or three); always ready to sit by the stove with her of a winter's evening, hanging on every word of her wonderfully rambling stories.

As Anne grows into a tall, graceful young woman, Marilla notices the changes and begins to articulate the feelings she has kept hidden—to all but the most discerning eye—within her fortress of propriety. Astonished to find Anne suddenly taller than herself, less inclined to chatter; even, apparently, too mature for her story club, Marilla finally gives way to tears as she realizes that Anne is about to leave Green Gables, if only for a year at Queen's.

"I just couldn't help thinking of the little girl you used to be, Anne. And I was wishing you could have stayed a little girl, even with all your queer ways...."

But Matthew need not undergo this shock of realization; in his silent way, he has always understood the essential Anne, " 'not a bit changed—not really,' " as she tells Marilla consolingly.

"The real me—back here—is just the same. It won't make a bit of difference where I go or how much I change outwardly; at heart I shall always be your little Anne, who will love you and Matthew and dear Green Gables more and better every day of her life."

Glowing light lends a delicate sweetness to the tiny downstairs chamber where Matthew Cuthbert lived.

And now the three of them are together for the summer. Anne is home from Queen's—bound for Redmond in September—and she's just had a lovely stroll with Matthew the evening before, through Lovers' Lane to the back pasture, lingering in the woods "all gloried through with sunset."

An impulse to go upstairs overwhelms me, so I take one last look around the kitchen for Matthew, then climb up to Anne's room where she and Marilla comforted each other after the loss of their beloved Matthew.

"He'd always been such a good, kind brother to me—"
"Oh, Marilla, what will we do without him?"
"We've got each other, Anne. I don't know what I'd do if you weren't here—"

Matthew is gone, wrenched away by that most relentless of killers—money. The bank in which he had faithfully kept his life's savings has failed, and the shock of this news proves to be too much for his weak heart—such a sad irony in those words, applied to someone overflowing with love.

Sleeping somewhere in the house are Anne and Marilla's good friends, the Barrys and Mrs. Lynde. And in the parlour the saddest of that chamber's formalities is being carried out: Matthew's body lies in a coffin, surrounded by flowers Anne has gathered.

I don't want to go in there. Not that I'm afraid. I just want to think of Matthew as Anne did yesterday while they walked—a memory she recalled this evening to bring forth tears in the desert of her silent anguish.

She could see Matthew's face smiling at her as he had smiled when they parted at the gate that last evening—she could hear his voice saying, "My girl—my girl that I'm proud of." Then the tears came and Anne wept her heart out.

Another Story

"The Bend in the Road." That's the title of the last chapter of *Anne of Green Gables*. A book's final chapter is usually a sad place to reach. You *do* discover how it all comes out but the thrill of resolution is no match for that empty feeling of turning the last page and forcing yourself to accept that there's no more to read. As Diana says, while she and Anne look down at the little schoolhouse at the close of term and the end of Miss Stacy's sojourn in Avonlea, " 'It does seem as if it was the end of everything, doesn't it?' "

But *Anne*'s last chapter is a bit different. The title itself suggests continuity; a life will take some twists and turns along the way, but it will follow its route, pre-ordained or chosen, depending on our beliefs. For Anne and Marilla, there have already been some twists and turns—not all of them pleasant, by any means. Fresh from their grief over Matthew's death, they learn that Marilla's eyesight is failing and that Green Gables must be sold; she can no longer look after the house, nor can she afford to hire help—all their savings have been lost in the bank's demise. At least Anne has a scholarship for Redmond, even if

The wooded hollow behind Avonlea school—or Cavendish school, as we move out of Anne Shirley's realm and into the world of her creator, Lucy Maud Montgomery.

she won't have a home to come to for vacations...

And here comes the *real* bend in the road; none of that is going to happen! Anne has spent a sleepless night alone with her doubts and fears, and comes up with a solution. She's going to stay at Green Gables.

> *"Oh, Anne, I could get on real well if you were here, I know. But I can't let you sacrifice yourself so for me. It would be terrible."*
>
> *"Nonsense!" Anne laughed merrily. "There is no sacrifice. Nothing could be worse than giving up Green Gables—nothing could hurt me more. We must keep the dear old place. My mind is quite made up, Marilla. I'm not going to Redmond; and I am going to stay here and teach. Don't you worry about me a bit."*

Everything falls into place. Anne wins a teaching post at Avonlea school; the position has been offered to Gilbert Blythe, but he gives it up and proposes the trustees choose Anne instead. And this last honourable effort on his part prompts Anne to finally forgive Gilbert—although perhaps Marilla's instructive story about *her* failure to forgive Gilbert's father after a similar spat also contributes to her decision.

In any event, they become friends at last, and as the book draws to a close there is a definite impression of love on the horizon. I imagine the two of them meeting some afternoon in the wooded hollow near the school, as of old; only now they're both teachers, he at White Sands, she here in Avonlea, and...

That's another story, though. And there *is* another story. There are several other books full of them, in fact—which is why *Anne of Green Gables* seems not so much to come to an end as, well, take a bend in the road.

> *"I don't know what lies around the bend, but I'm going to believe the best does. It has a fascination of its own, that bend, Marilla. I wonder how the road beyond it goes—what there is of green glory and soft, checkered lights and shadows—what new landscapes— what new beauties—what curves and hills and valleys farther on."*

∽

Wild rose bushes line the border of
the picket fence beyond the path at
Green Gables.

The one-room schoolhouse is long gone,
but the brook still ripples gently in the
hollow behind the place where the building
once stood. Students repaired to the hollow
at recess and lunchtime—all but Maud,
who had to go home for dinner.

At the School Hollow

As I fondly gaze at the hollow near the school where Maud's classmates spent their happy noontimes without her, a flock of birds flutter down to feed among the foilage in the hollow. Magically, the image re-arranges itself into a group of young girls lounging in the heat of a summer's day on the moss covered banks of the brook. All about them, amidst the bushes, ferns, and rocks of the hollow, lies scattered the evidence of that time-honoured tradition called "playing house"— chipped and broken cups and saucers carefully laid on shelflike, green-tufted stones after being filled with luscious summer berries and clear, fresh spring water.

"Let's make rainbows!" calls one of the children, a slender, rather pale girl whose limpid, soulful eyes set off her delicate, pointed face. At once the others leap to their feet and join her in plucking twigs from the long-suffering balsam firs that line the hollow. These, well coated with the sticky resin that gives this evergreen its name, are carefully set adrift in the brook where, light as bark, they bob merrily along the fast-moving stream, the droplets on their surfaces catching the sun and tossing it into the air in a kaleidoscope of nature that never fails to elicit an "Ah!" of wonder—even though the young onlookers have seen the colourful spectacle a hundred times before.

As they hover over the brook, enraptured with their tiny, rainbow-hued boats, I notice—even as Matthew noticed, watching Anne practise for *The Fairy Queen* with her friends at Green Gables—that the dreamy-eyed child who proposed the game seems different from her companions. They're all wearing light, breezy pinafores and going barefoot, while she, even in the summer's heat, wears big, heavy, black-laced shoes—more like boots, really—and a dark little dress whose style seems more suited to a six-year-old than a girl of, what, eleven? Twelve?

I can tell by the long, flowing dark hair that it's not Anne, though that voice, exclaiming in delight as a particularly brilliant little vessel sails past, carries "clear, sweet" tones very like those described in the book, very like those I've heard on my journey through Anne's world; though her eyes are as bright and full of visions, her mouth as "sweet-lipped and expressive"—

It *must* be Maud—Lucy Maud Montgomery herself! And that would be Amanda at her side. I smile, remembering Maud's account of how the two girls became friends—luscious, ripe apples from her grandparents' orchard, offered to Amanda's desk-mates at school, won Maud the right to take their place at her side. Maud and Amanda sat together throughout their time at Cavendish school, and remained best friends for years. As Maud recalled in her journals, "Not a bad bargain for four apples!!!"

Suddenly the tinkling of a bell interrupts my musings. The girls rise up in a flutter, like so many wild swans, and fly back towards the schoolhouse.

A Dear Little House

I leave the hollow and make my way back to Highway 13. It's time to say good-bye to tea parties and rainbows, for the moment, and begin a new journey, through the world of Lucy Maud Montgomery. Of course, as we've just discovered, Anne's and Maud's paths frequently intersect—they are, in many significant ways, one and the same person—but there are equally important distinctions, just as there are between stories and real life. Yet I sense the two will intertwine again before long.

As I wend my way along the winding road west from Cavendish, the misty morning sky evokes a reflective mood, tinged with melancholy. Although the village where I'm headed is where Maud first drew breath—and thus a place of joy and hope—it is also a place of great sorrow, where a desperately ill young wife and mother was forced to confront the awful reality that she would never see her baby daughter bloom into a happy girl, an accomplished young woman, a bride. And more terrible still, her child would have to grow up without a mother.

I try to banish these thoughts from my mind as I reach the village and find the little house at the crossroads, where Hugh John Montgomery and Clara Woolner Macneill moved just after they were married in March 1874. It is a dear little house—more like a cottage, really—surrounded by lush green bushes and trees. How happy they must have been for those first few months here: Hugh, then thirty-two and a prosperous merchant whose wholesale and retail trade with the West Indies was thriving, also operated a general store, Clifton House, right next door; and Clara, only twenty-one, excitedly awaited the birth of her first—as it turned out, her only—child.

That child, born in the little east room upstairs, on the last day of November, was named Lucy Maud, Lucy for her maternal grandmother and "Maud for herself," as Mollie Gillen writes in *The Wheel of Things*.

For years after she grew up, Maud was drawn to revisit the little house in Clifton (now New London), where she was born but spent only the first year of her life.

She would only live in this house for a short time, but its emotional importance to her would never wane. Today, it is painted white with green trim, and the village is called New London; but otherwise the house stands relatively unchanged since Maud wrote about it in her journal many decades ago:

Beyond Stanley the road wound to another little village—Clifton. And here, around a certain corner, is a certain small, yellowish-brown house, close to the road, that I always look at with a certain kind of fascination, for it is the house where my father and mother lived after their marriage and where I was born and spent the first year of my life. The years have passed on and each succeeding one has left the little brown house something shabbier than before, but its enchantment has never faded in my eyes. I always look for it with the same eager interest when I turn the corner....

I move from room to room as if in a dream, glancing at the memorabilia of Maud's life displayed here—her wedding dress, family photographs, albums filled with stories and poems, scrapbooks crammed with keepsakes. *Just like Anne,* I think, smiling; *she kept everything.*

Climbing the narrow stairs to the room where she was born, I become anxious with anticipation. *What will I see? How will I feel?* As I stand in the doorway peering in, the sun breaks through the clouds and sends rays of light through the open window. The room glows with warmth.

"I do wish she'd lived long enough for me to remember calling her mother. I think it would be sweet to say 'mother,' don't you?"

Transfixed, I let Anne's words—Maud's words—course through me, as achingly tender as that unaccountable burst of sunlight.

Fields and Flowers

It has always seemed to me, ever since early childhood, that, amid all the commonplaces of life, I was very near a kingdom of ideal beauty. Between it and me hung only a thin veil. I could never draw it quite aside, but sometimes a wind fluttered it and I caught a glimpse of the enchanting realm beyond—only a glimpse, but those glimpses always made life worthwhile.

Pressed flowers, ribbons, and printed prose and verses; —Maud kept everything.

Maud revelled in the beauty of the fields, streams, and woods on her grandparents' property in Cavendish.

John Macneill and his wife, Margaret Simpson, one of the five families that founded Cavendish, settled on five hundred acres bordering the community's north shore—quite a generous tract of land considering the relatively small size of Prince Edward Island in general and the area surrounding this seaside settlement in particular. The Macneills, Maud's great-great-grandparents, also founded something of a dynasty of large families dedicated to the growth of the fledgling community and the well-being of the homestead; Maud's great-grandfather, William Macneill, served as Speaker of the province's House of Assembly as well as farming the family lands, and his son Alexander, also a farmer, inherited the homestead and also acted as Cavendish postmaster.

It was with Alexander Macneill and his wife, Lucy Ann Woolner, that Maud came to live during the last few months of her mother's life; the old homestead would become her home until her grandmother's death, more than three decades later. Growing up amidst all this history, handed down by her mother's family with the frequent wit and knack for story-

telling exemplified by many of her relatives, you would think that Maud would have developed a strong sense of ownership—a proprietary interest—concerning the Macneill holdings.

Indeed, she cherished the fields, full of waving wheat in summer and autumn, and wildflowers in spring; the "Dear Old Trees" bordering them; the old rambling paths down to the sea. Yet this affection, like all our finest feelings, rested not so much in a sense of possession as in a yielding to beauty—an openness to the wonders of nature, which affords us a "glimpse of the enchanting realm," as Maud expressed it in "The Alpine Path." Or, as William Blake said:

> *He who binds to himself a joy*
> *Does the winged life destroy;*
> *But he who kisses the joy as it flies*
> *Lives in eternity's sunrise.*

As I walk through the golden grain in the field near the site of the old homestead, a feeling of serenity fills me. The stalks of wheat rustle softly in the sun, which is warm but not overpowering; and from far away I can hear a sweet voice singing—the soloist in the Cavendish United Church.

Yet, mingled with the tranquillity and beauty of the scene is a sadness that becomes almost palpable. I reflect on the child Maud, and the words she wrote, years later, in a letter to her fellow writer and frequent correspondent G.B. Macmillan. "I was a lonely child. Orphaned by the

The bells of Cavendish United Church (formerly the Presbyterian church where Maud's husband Ewan was once minister) can easily be heard from the fields surrounding the Macneill homestead.

early death of my mother…I had no companionship except that of books and solitary rambles in the wood and fields. This drove me in on myself and early forced me to construct for myself a world of fancy and imagination very different indeed from the world in which I lived, moved and had my outward being."

No child should be lonely, I tell myself.

How different it all would have been if Maud's mother had lived! Or would it? Was it enforced isolation alone that gave rise to Maud's extraordinary imagination, the "world of fancy" where she found Anne? Is it possible that she would have sought that solitary world in any case, living in a place as beautiful as this and gifted with an artist's perception such as hers, a sensibility so nourished by nature? Or could the strict rules of the Macneill household have actually promoted her development as a writer by providing her, however harshly, with more of an incentive to create than might have existed in a "normal" home.

But that loneliness! For Maud, as cheerful and gregarious as she was contemplative and self-directed, the separation from youthful society and its pleasures was clearly excruciating. Would it really have made her a lesser artist if she had been freer to enjoy the company and activities of young people her own age?

Only the wind answers me. It sounds like the murmuring of a child's cry.

The Foundation and the Fantasy

My mixed feelings about Maud's life with the Macneills follow me down the path to the stone foundation of the family homestead. Although the day is clear and bright, the air hangs heavy—or is that just the weight of what I'm feeling?—and even the lovely tree-lined route I'm taking seems little relief for the oppressiveness that grows stronger as I approach what remains of the old homestead, torn down about ten years after the death of Maud's grandmother in 1911.

What's left of the "old-fashioned Cavendish farmhouse, surrounded by apple orchards," which Maud described in "The Alpine Path," is a rectangular, rock-enclosed excavation surrounding a smaller block of stones, topped with spruce saplings poking pertly from the cracks.

The rigidity of the scene in unavoidably symbolic. Out of the neatly stacked piles of rock rises the image of two decidedly formal, icy personages in their mid-fifties, reproving fingers ready to wag at the slightest evidence of impulsive behaviour. Alexander Marquis Macneill, farmer and postmaster, often away from the house because of his farming duties—bossy, critical, and irritable when at home. Lucy Ann Woolner

Macneill, reserved to the point of coldness, and, Maud recalls in her journals, "domineering and narrow-minded" in her attitude to others, especially the little girl whose care she undertook after her own daughter's death.

For much of her early childhood she had no friends at all; later, those few she was permitted were rarely invited to the Macneill home— and as for social functions such as parties, they were entirely out of the question. It's true that for a time she had two playmates who were *always* at the house—the Nelson boys—but their three years together provided only a brief respite for Maud, in the context of a highly circumscribed childhood, youth, and even adulthood (she was well over thirty when her grandmother died).

Yet there are other images here, evoked when I begin to think of this foundation not merely as cold, unyielding stone, but as a representation of hearth and home. The substance of life.

Although she received much more emotional sustenance from her relatives at Park Corner, whom she visited frequently, the Macneills gave Maud a permanent home and "in material respects they were good and kind." And if they were generally undemonstrative, her grandparents did occasionally unbend just a little. Maud remembered for years her grandfather's account of the legend of Cape Leforce. This rocky spot was named for a French sea-captain killed in a sunrise duel after a quarrel with his mate over the booty seized from an English ship off the coast of what would become Cavendish. The captain, Maud recalled in

The old Macneill homestead, first settled by Maud's great-great-grandparents, was demolished about ten years after the death of Lucy Macneill, Maud's grandmother. Only the foundation remains.

"The Alpine Path," "was buried by his crew on the spot where he fell, and I have often heard Grandfather say that *his* father had seen the grave in his boyhood."

"It has long ago crumbled into the waves, but the name still clings to the red headland."

Not only a gifted storyteller, Alexander Macneill was also "a man of strong and pure literary tastes, with a considerable knack of prose composition," Maud wrote in "The Alpine Path." And his wife was a highly intelligent woman, well schooled and well read. Two of Grandfather Macneills' brothers wrote poetry, and the sitting-room library was always well stocked with an abundance of verse and a rather more judiciously selected collection of prose, (hardly a shock, considering the Macneills' strong sense of propriety).

The world of books, a sequestered life, a literary family—the right soil for producing a writer. But the intense emotional power of her writing, with its enchanting, absorbing narratives and vivid descriptions, owes its origins to more than the Macneill literary tradition. Everywhere she found herself, whether grappling with a difficult, often painful life at the Macneills', or enjoying a welcome respite with her father's family at Park Corner, or at school, or wandering along the coastlines and wooded paths she loved so well, Maud would transform her experience—unpleasant or delightful—through the gift of her transcendent imagination.

Upbringing, genetics, the work of a higher power—who really knows where such gifts come from? What is most important is that Maud made the most of what she was given, even before she began writing seriously. If her stern grandparents would not share her abundant love, she bestowed it upon her room—"my dear old room," as she later called it. Or upon the fields, streams, and woods outside. And through the transformative power of fiction, she rewrote her own story by giving even the repressed Marilla the tiny chink in her armour through which Anne's affection, vitality, and passion for nature could penetrate.

Marilla looked at her with a tenderness that would never have been suffered to reveal itself in any clearer light than that soft mingling of fireshine and shadow. The lesson of a love that should display itself easily in spoken word and open look was one Marilla could never learn. But she had learned to love this slim, grey-eyed girl with an affection all the deeper and stronger from its very undemonstrativeness.

Late-afternoon shadows have begun to fall, softening the harsh, fortresslike angles of the Macneill foundation. I've been so deep in thought that I haven't even noticed the shift in the light. And it must be that tricky light, for up there on the highest part of the structure, it looks like someone is sitting.

Could it be the pale little dark-haired girl again, whom I've come to know as Maud? She doesn't know about Anne or Marilla, which isn't surprising, because she hasn't invented them yet. But she's certainly practising: what she has invented in an imaginary playmate, since real ones are denied her.

And I do believe she and her friend are together now. Maud is smiling, reaching out toward-someone. Suddenly, I remember Katie Maurice—Maud wrote about her in "The Alpine Path."

> *In our sitting-room there had always stood a big book-case used as a china cabinet. In each door was a large oval glass, dimly reflecting the room. When I was very small each of my reflections in these glass doors were real folk to my imagination. The one in the left-hand door was Katie Maurice....Katie Maurice was a little girl like myself, and I loved her dearly. I would stand for hours, giving and receiving confidences.*

Someday you will write about her, Maud, I whisper. Someday she will be the invisible friend of an immortal creation of yours—Anne Shirley.

Now kept in the parlour of the Campbell house in Park Corner, home of Maud's Uncle John and family, this bookcase once stood in the Macneill home, where Maud found her imaginary friend Katie in the left-hand glass door.

Treasured memories from Maud's scrapbook, a page dedicated to cats and kittens, including tuffs of fur, tied with a ribbon and bow, from one of Maud's beloved cats!

Dolls and Kittens

Besides her imaginary playmates, little Maud always enjoyed playing out in the old homestead orchard, with her dolls and kittens. Her doll family, which included three wax and two china, were each christened with "fancy" names. The wax dolls came in various sizes; one as large as a "real" baby, one as small as a child's stocking, which was where Maud discovered her on Christmas morning, and one "just right!" because she wore the most beautiful dress imaginable, red cashmere and lace. Then there were the two china dolls, one with a broken head, the other missing an arm. Maud always gave extra attention to her poor unfortunated dolls, and "…loved them for their very misfortunes!"

Quite near the old foundation, lovingly supported by a wooden brace, grows Maud's old apple tree. Here, in days gone-by, she played beneath it's branches, arranging her dolls, furniture, and china tea set upon an old quilt. With each season, Maud's cherished apple tree brought new wonders and delights: in spring its blossoms drifted down upon her, in summer its cool leafy canopy sheltered her, and in fall she feasted on the bounty of its harvest.

Ever since Maud could remember, "She loved cats!" Her grandparents "detested them" but never prevented Maud from playing with them. She soon adopted two of the cutest little kittens on the farm and named them "Pussywillow" and "Catkin." Pussywillow had a fur of gray strips, Catkin the pinkest-nose. Often, they would join Maud and the dolls on the old quilt. (I'm almost sure that Maud dressed up the kittens in the doll's bonnets and bibs, like I once did, and like my daughter did also.)

Throughout the summer, the kittens slept in the granary, and by fall they were old enough to roam the barns freely at night.

"But one bitter morning," Maud painstakingly relates in her journals, "I found Pussywillow dying of poison, caused by eating a poisoned rat. My little pet died in my hands. Never shall I forget the agony!"

"It was the first time I realized death—the first time anything I really loved left me forever…It is twenty five years later since that day and the scar of that hurt is still on my soul."

Maud, eleven years old, so devastated by the death of her kitten that she mourned for months. Sometimes she dreamed that Pussywillow was still alive, but when she awoke the reality of his death was painfully real. Perhaps the reason Maud spent so much time grieving the death of her beloved kitten, was because she never had an opportunity, being only twenty-one months old, to mourn the death of her mother.

Good Times at Park Corner

Uncle John Campbell's house was a big white one, smothered in orchards. Here, in other days, there was a trio of merry cousins to rush out and drag me in with greeting and laughter. The very walls of this house must have been permeated by the essence of good times.

> —Lucy Maud Montgomery, "The Alpine Path," *Everywoman's World*

Only about thirteen miles along the rugged Gulf of St. Lawrence coast from Cavendish lies the picturesque little community of Park Corner. Its rolling hills, gurgling streams, tranquil ponds, and spectacular shoreline create a landscape every bit as beautiful as that of Cavendish, yet in another sense this place constitutes a completely different world. Lucy Maud Montgomery viewed this, her father's birthplace and the home town of his family for many generations, as a release from the constricting life her maternal grandparents imposed on her.

And I, exploring the pathways of Maud's world, feel the lightening of her load the moment I turn away from the Macneill foundation and begin my journey to Silver Bush, the Campbell home. (The Campbells and Montgomerys joined families many generations ago, and the Campbells were also directly connected with the Macneills—Aunt Annie, John Campbell's wife, was an older sister of Maud's mother.)

Oh, I know this is no black-and-white equation of cruel grandparents on the one side and kindly uncles and cousins on the other: joy and laughter with young people her own age will come to Maud's life in Cavendish, and she will come to deeply value, if not emotionally resonate with, the stability and intellectual structure the Macneills offer.

But children (and adults, too,) need to play as surely as they need food and clothes and education. The nourishment of play—that's what Maud found at Silver Bush; and as I drive up to the big white farmhouse, I can feel the happiness fairly glimmer in the warm summer light. I wander into the fields and woods behind the house, drawn by the bell-like peals of childish laughter. Clara, Stella, and Fredericka Campbell (the "trio of merry cousins") are out with Maud for a blissful afternoon of berry-picking and rambling "through wooded lanes fragrant with June-bells, threaded with sunshine and shadow, carpeted with mosses, where we saw foxes and rabbits in their native haunts."

Unlike the Macneill property, where the joy of Maud's childhood exploration stopped at the portal—to be replaced by solitary fantasies in sitting-room or bedroom—the Campbell homestead offered shared enjoyment both outdoors and within. I wander from room to room, marvelling at how the elegant formality of the furnishings is enlivened by the years of happiness that were spent here. Maud's words, written later in her journals, echo through the house:

Each room has its memories—the kitchen where we toasted our toes at the glowing old 'Waterloo,' the front rooms where we spent

Trips to Park Corner were doubly pleasant for Maud—Grandfather Montgomery on one side of the road, the Campbells on the other.

so many jolly evenings, the big bedrooms upstairs where we slept and talked; and best of all, that famous old pantry, stored with good things, into which it was our habit to crowd at bedtime and gnaw bones, crunch fruitcake and scream with laughter.

As I peer into the pantry, I can hear that delightful laughter again, imagine Maud and her cousins in their little white nightgowns, their small bare feet pattering on the floor as they poke through the well-stocked shelves for a late-night treat. These images proceed me upstairs as I look for the room where Maud stayed many years later while awaiting the day of her wedding to the Reverend Macdonald.

I try to see her all grown up, by the glass, a glowing bride-to-be, cooling her cheek against the bouquet of lilies-of-the-valley and white roses, arranging her necklace of amethysts and pearls, a gift from her intended. But the image does not arise before my eyes, as it has with the child Maud and her friends—or the child Anne.

She's not there yet, I tell myself, slowly descending the stairs. *Let her be a child a little longer. The time goes fast enough....*

Down in the beautifully furnished, inviting parlour, the glow of early evening spreads its palette of rose and lavender across soft cushions, smooth brocade, gleaming wood—Oh! There it is; the bookcase with the oval glass doors! Katie Maurice's residence, now here at the Campbell home, where Maud so loved to play. An ideal destination, I whisper to myself, approaching the lovely antique. I'm too tall to see my whole

At dawn, the silver stillness of the Campbell pond makes it easy to see why Maud chose this as the primary source for her description of Anne's Lake of Shining Waters.

reflection in the glass, and besides, the colours of twilight are taking up most of the two ovals, so I start thinking about taking my leave when suddenly the colours recede. In their place I can see the images of two children.

The one in the left-hand door—Katie's door—is the unmistakably Titian-topped Anne.

The other is Maud, head tilted, listening intently to Anne.

"I used to talk to her by the hour, especially on Sunday, and tell her everything. Katie was the comfort and consolation of my life. We used to pretend that the bookcase was enchanted and that if I only knew the spell I could open the door and step right into the room where Katie Maurice lived...."

I wheel around to try to catch a glimpse of the girls who *have* to be standing in the room looking at themselves in the mirrorlike doors, but—shouldn't I have expected it?—the room is empty. Except for me.

Shining Lakes, Enchanted Dogs

Up before dawn, I pick my way through the trees that lead to the banks of the Campbell pond. I want to be there at sunrise to capture the image of the first rays dancing across this special place of enchantment—Maud's prototype for the pond Anne named the Lake of Shining Waters. I've already expressed my rather arbitrary preference for the Cavendish pond as Anne's shining lake—and Maud herself did acknowledge its influence on the delineation of its contours, and on the hilltop perspective from which Anne first sees it. Besides, my logical half tells me, the lake of Shining Waters is in Avonlea—and that's Cavendish, not Park Corner!

But of course stories don't work quite that straightforwardly. Characters are composites: Maud and Anne have strikingly similar personalities, but Maud didn't grow up in an orphanage and Anne didn't write twenty novels. So it goes, too, with the places of fiction: the Lake of Shining Waters holds the best of both worlds—the vantage point of Green Gables in Cavendish, the gleaming expanse of unbroken silver here in Park Corner.

And there is the sun, edging its way out over the tops of the trees across the water, which shines so brightly it's as if it is trying to earn sole rights to the name!

Over on the opposite bank awaits the other main attraction of Maud's visits to Park Corner—the Montgomery homestead. This is the birthplace of Maud's father, whose forbears settled in Prince Edward Island in 1769—like the Macneills, an industrious and determined family of farmers and, later, community leaders and politicians.

Just *how* determined? Apparently, Maud's great-great-grandfather Hugh Montgomery and his family had intended to settle in Quebec, but when their ship stopped off the Island for water, Hugh's wife, Mary MacShannon, went ashore to seek relief from seasickness—and refused to get back on the boat. As historian Francis W.P. Bolger puts it in *The Years Before "Anne,"* "Prince Edward Island is grateful that a woman's strong will prevailed."

Lucy Maud Montgomery was certainly grateful as well: she adored her paternal grandfather, Donald Montgomery—later Senator Montgomery—and treasured her memories of visits to the "quaint and delightful" old house on the family farm. Before her father took up permanent residence in Prince Albert in 1881, he often accompanied her to Park Corner on his frequent trips back to the Island from out west. These were very special times for the motherless little girl: surrounded by "a grandfather out of a story book....good and kind and gentle," and her much-cherished father—"the most lovable man I ever met"—she spent many of her happiest days exploring the "cupboards and nooks, and little, unexpected corners" of the big, rambling farmhouse.

After Hugh Montgomery finally settled in Saskatchewan, first as a realtor and auctioneer, later in various government, railway, and insurance posts, his daughter continued to visit Park Corner regularly. In many ways, Grandfather Montgomery became a surrogate for the father who was just not there enough—and who, by all accounts, had some difficulties during his career that must have made him seem even more inaccessible to his young daughter. He went out of business twice, and while working for the Crown Timber Office in Prince Albert, he was reprimanded for "making remarks" against his superior officer, one D.J. Waggoner; he was transferred to Battleford for five years.

The long absences, the deprecating remarks about her early literary efforts, the business woes—none of it seemed to shake the steadfastness of her affections. Even his remarriage, and to a woman twenty years his junior, did nothing to undermine her love. Perhaps she was displaying the same sort of determination evinced by her ancestors; or perhaps the relatively few experiences father and daughter shared at the Montgomery house proved more significant than the many miles between them.

Yet Maud knew he was not the ideal father, or she probably would have written more of him into the character of Matthew Cuthbert, whose kind, gentle ways with his beloved Anne bear more resemblance to Maud's memories of Grandfather Montgomery or Uncle John Campbell. Matthew's shy, introverted nature brings to mind Maud's description of her elderly cousin David Macneill—who, like the fictional Matthew, owned Green Gables.

Yet the essential Matthew incorporates a simplicity of spirit and a selflessness of love that transcend the character traits of any of Maud's

Maud's father told her that, come midnight, the two spotted china dogs on the mantel in the Montgomery sitting-room would come to life.

male relatives, while borrowing a bit from all of them—just as the deep but hidden love Marilla feels for Anne hints at what Maud might have hoped for in Grandmother Macneill, but which was (unlike Marilla's) never clearly expressed.

Still, there was clearly love between Hugh John Montgomery and his daughter....

As I enter the sitting-room of the lovely, tree-shaded home at Park Corner, I notice the large spotted china dog on the gleaming mantelpiece. Its mouth is open, as if ready to let out a mighty woof, and I'm reminded of a story Maud's father once told about these dogs—that they come to life on the stroke of midnight, jump down onto the hearth,

and start barking. So struck was she by this tale that years later, on her honeymoon trip—and more than a decade after his death—Maud bought a similar pair of dogs in a shop in York, England.

Articulated Love

With a much lighter heart than I carried with me after my vigil at the Macneill foundation, I return to Cavendish to explore further the world in which Maud spent most of her childhood and youth. Tomorrow I will return to the fields and woods around her grandparents' farmhouse—playgrounds that would eventually echo with childish laughter other than her own—but there is a place I am moved to visit first.

Revisit, I should say, since I have already spent many wonderful hours exploring Lovers' Lane, and Balsam Hollow beyond it—those wondrous places around the fictional, and the real, Green Gables. Named by the historical child Maud and by the storybook child Anne, they nourish the spirit with that particular grace lent by sacred sites.

Nature abounds everywhere in Maud's world, from the dunes of the coastline to the ponds and hills, the fields and woods and winding pathways of the interior. She knew and loved it all, but there was a special place in her heart for the path below Green Gables; the brook nestled amidst grasses, ferns, and wild-rose bushes; the hollow thick with evergreens and maples, and the air "dripping with fragrance—dying fir, frosted ferns, wet leaves," as she recalls.

Always made welcome by David and Margaret Macneill, the brother and sister—as were Matthew and Marilla Cuthbert—who owned the now-fabled farmhouse, Maud often visited Green Gables, and especially its surroundings, as a child. These sojourns won her grandparents' approval, since it *was* her relatives' home that Maud was visiting; and it was on one of her rambles with the Macneills' youthful boarders, Wellington and David Nelson, that Maud discovered Lovers' Lane and Balsam Hollow.

When Maud came to write *Anne of Green Gables,* although she meticulously reproduced the natural setting and exterior appearance of the house and barn, the interiors bore little resemblance to the Macneill siblings' home. Instead, she based Matthew and Marilla's parlour and kitchen, sitting-room and bedrooms upon the furnishings of her grandparents' house—again, perhaps, hoping that transplanting their highly structured lives to an environment where nature, as well as the influence of an emotional force like Anne, would open them—symbolically if not in real life—to the possibilities of articulated love.

As I leave the hollow to return to Lovers' Lane, the sun is just setting. Now I have been here at dawn, noon, and dusk, I realize, wondering at this newest glimpse of beauty, this twilight sifting its fine shadows like opalescent grains of sand through the scarlet glow. I hear Maud's voice,

Lovers' Lane, Balsam Hollow, and all the other enchantingly lovely places around Green Gables were a fairy-tale playground to young Maud—and she never outgrew them.

see through Anne's eyes as she brings the cows in from pasture...

> *...all the gaps and clearings in the woods were brimmed up with ruby sunset light. Here and there the lane was splashed with it, but for the most part it was already quite shadowy beneath the maples, and the spaces under the firs were filled with a clear violet dusk like airy wine.*

Green Gables is shrouded in the fast-falling darkness as I approach—but in the window of the east gable room, a tiny light is shining, symbol of hope, symbol of home and hearth, and symbol of Anne's cherished friendship with Diana. I gaze out into the velvety evening, its hush broken only by the sweet music of birds and crickets.

From far off in the distance comes a flickering light. It can't be Diana

signalling back—it's *can't!* It's probably a firefly. Besides, it's not coming from Orchard Slope at all; it's coming from over *there,* near the old school....The Macneill property, I suddenly realize. *Maud, Maud, is that you?*

A light shines in the east gable window until ten at night, commemorating the signalling system Anne and Diana devised to send messages between Green Gables and Orchard Slope.

A Room of Her Own

Rejuvenated and inspired after my latest visit to Lovers' Lane and Balsam Hollow, I rise early to return to the Macneill homestead. I've found out from the descendants of Maud's grandparents, who still live on this land and graciously host pilgrims like myself, the location of the various rooms in the old house, relative to the foundation stones that are the only physical record. Thus informed, I try to re-create the perspective Maud might have had looking out the window of her beloved little room—where the pulsing light I saw yesterday evening seemed to come from.

Anne's life force transformed the small, stark chamber where she lived, so that it became a place filled with its own vitality—even when she wasn't there. Maud, her creator, infused her room at the Macneills' with so strong a sense of her own spirit that it took on a sacred quality, which could no more be extinguished by the wrecker's ball than the soul can be destroyed by death.

For writers, especially women, a sense of exclusive space is paramount—the "room of one's own" Virginia Woolf describes so passionately in her book of the same title. For Lucy Maud Montgomery, her room was a place of retreat from her ambivalent and often painful relationship with her grandparents, a place to reflect upon her experiences at school or explorations of the natural world, a place to read, to dream, and especially to write. Maud's room was her watchtower onto the world, as she wrote in her journals:

> *It is a veritable little haven of rest and dreams to me, and the window opens on a world of wonder and beauty. Winds drift by with clover scent in their breath; the rustle of leaves comes up from the poplars, and birds flit low in joyous vagrance. Below is a bosky old apple orchard and a row of cherry trees along the dyke where the old tamarack stands guard.*

I gaze across the field; the landscape is quite different now, yet the words are so vivid that it takes little effort to see those trees—and I'm sure the spicy scent of clover pierces as sharply as it did then. Here, too, is the "star-dusted valley of buttercups, and the blue, blue sky

> *that at sunset will be curtained with wonderful splendours, and at night will be thick-sown with stars and at dawn will be washed with silver and sheen and radiance.*

In front of the foundation wall, I sit down for a moment and, like a child, picture myself leaping up in the air to capture the perspective of height—imagine myself into Maud's vanished room. There is a quick flash of casement, white muslin, and the girlish Maud peering out eagerly—the lonely look I have grown used to replaced by a smile as brilliant as this sunshine.

Then she is gone, and the room is gone too, before I've even had the chance to let my eyes linger over bedstead and table and chest, and especially over the flowers I am sure she always had nearby, for Maud loved flowers, "the sweetest things God ever made."

And she loved her little room, too, "more than I ever loved another place on earth...."

When finally Maud left the old homestead, after the publication of *Anne of Green Gables* in 1908, after her grandmother's death three years later, and just before her marriage, she recalls, in her journals:

> *I cried myself to sleep in the cold darkness—and thus was passed my last night in that old beloved white room, where I had dreamed my dreams of girlhood and suffered the heartaches of lonely womanhood, where I had written my best, where I had endured my defeats, and exulted in my victories. Never again was I to lay my*

The view from the window of Lucy Maud Montgomery's "little haven of rest and dreams"—her bedroom at the Macneill homestead—would have looked something like this.

head on its pillow there—never again waken to see the morning sunshine gleaming in at the little, muslin-curtained window where I had knelt so many nights since childhood to pray beneath the stars.

How Sunflowers Survive

The ancient trees surrounding the foundation stones look like giant sentries keeping watch over this sacred site. For watchguards, though, they seem surprisingly friendly—strong and serene, but not in the least threatening, and there's even a feeling of playfulness about their curlicued branches and huge canopies of green.

It's as if these trees could remember a time when three children chattered and laughed beneath their boughs like so many joyous robins, all bounce and comical tilt of heads and merry sparkle of innocent young eyes.

Wellington Nelson was eight years old—Maud's age—when he and his seven-year-old brother, David, came to live at the Macneill house for three years while attending Cavendish school. The boys, whose parents were dead, had been living with an aunt, whose home was too far away

Like giant sentinels standing guard over a site made sacred by its memories, these old trees cast vivid patterns of light and shadow over the Macneill property.

for them to get to and from school. It was common practice in those days for youngsters to board with families in communities that had their own schoolhouses.

Well and Dave, as Maud soon nicknamed her new friends, showed as intense a love as she for the wonders and delights of Cavendish's woods, fields, streams, and, of course, sea. Every moment not spent in school was devoted to the exploration of this outdoor playground.

Out among these sentinel trees was once a little garden that the children tended, planting seeds, watering, and meticulously yanking out every weed. Alas, their over-attention proved to be its undoing— except for a few hardy sunflowers over in a corner, which flourished because of the children's neglect. But the plants failed to thrive.

Not so their friendship. Whether walking to and from school, visiting Lovers' Lane and the old log bridge behind Green Gables, or heading down to the beach to gather shells and hunks of driftwood—shaped like sea-creatures right out of a storybook—the three were inseparable.

Of course, Maud *did* manage to make time for her friends Amanda and Penzie, (also her cousins).

It seemed that the once-solitary little girl was being given at least a chance at something resembling a normal childhood, despite the early tragedies, the wrenching changes, and the emotional wilderness of her grandparents way of life.

I think again of the sunflowers in the children's garden. A light breeze rustles in the leaves of the noble trees around me.

The Spruce Grove

The Avonlea school was a whitewashed building low in the eaves and wide in the windows, furnished inside with comfortable substantial old-fashioned desks that opened and shut and were carved all over their lids with the initials and hieroglyphics of three generations of school-children.

Change the name Avonlea to Cavendish, and you'd be describing the place where Maud spent her school days—which in the 1880s meant going to class all year, with breaks in spring and fall for planting and harvesting, and a week off in July to commemorate Confederation Day (or Canada Day, as we call it now).

Like her alter ego, Anne Shirley, Lucy Maud Montgomery experienced a system of education that would be unrecognizable by those accustomed to the specialized classrooms of today. The one-room schoolhouse was presided over by a single teacher responsible for all grade levels and ages, and every subject from algebra to Latin. It was a position of great power, and if you were unlucky enough to get a cranky teacher like Anne's Mr. Phillips or a critical one like Maud's Miss Robinson, well, you had to make the best of it.

Maud loved the spruce grove near Cavendish school—a place of "better educative influence" than the classroom, she later said.

And make the best of it Maud did. Growing up in a literary house-hold, she was far ahead of her classmates in reading and writing when she started school at six, and she was quick to sample—then devour—all the new books she found in the library, memorizing whole passages and astounding even the exacting Miss Robinson with her talent for recitation—even as little Anne did in Avonlea.

Only a wooded lot now stands on the site of the Cavendish school, but as I peer through the thick spruce that line the road, I can almost—but not quite—make out the contours of the low-slung white building. But as before, I *can* hear the laughter of children, echoes from the past, in the woods down there in the hollow, by the brook where Anne and her friends "put their bottles of milk in the morning to keep cool and sweet until dinner-time."

As I make my way towards the peals of laughter, I suddenly remember that it was the participation in such rituals—and all the companion-ship they represented—that set Maud and Anne apart most sharply, and painfully. "Not for me," she recalled sadly in "The Alpine Path," was the pleasure of " 'scooting' down the winding path before school-time to put my bottle against a mossy log, where the sunlit water might dance and ripple against its creamy whiteness."

I lean against an old evergreen, suddenly overcome by sorrow. I know it was just a little bottle of milk, and Maud's friends still included her in their games at recess, but being wrenched away from her class-mates at lunchtime made her feel isolated, just as the very proper cloth-ing did, and the rules about attending social functions outside school and church....

How generous, and how optimistic of Maud to give Anne a place in the school brook for *her* bottle of milk. And how characteristic of her to revel in the positive influence of nature on the soul rather than focus solely on the pain of human relationships:

> *The old spruce grove, with its sprinkling of maple, was a fairy realm of beauty and romance to my childish imagination. I shall always be thankful that my school was near a grove, a place with winding paths and a treasure-trove of ferns and mosses and wood-flowers. It was a stronger and better educative influence in my life than the lessons learned at the desk in the school-house.*
> —*"The Alpine Path"*

With Well and Dave

With the arrival of the Nelson boys, Maud's solitary walks home at dinnertime came to an end. Not that she ever had far to go, geographi-cally speaking: the gate to the Macneill property was at the road across from the school building; well, the school was set back slightly from the road, but still, the trip to and from school took only a matter of minutes and had the added charm of leading the traveller along a lovely tree-lined path that started just outside the Macneill farmhouse.

Nevertheless, it must have seemed a difficult journey at times for the little girl, separated from her companions and their noontime games, facing a seemingly endless and no doubt highly formal meal in the sitting-room.

She still had to go home for dinner once Well and Dave came to live at the house—but so did they; not a case of misery loving company, exactly, but something similar. Maud was no longer the *only* pupil at Cavendish school who had to forgo the midday pleasures of the school hollow, and there were even days when the three children got back soon enough to join in the fun before the bell rang to signal the start of afternoon classes. Besides, there was always that wonderful few minutes before school started—or at recess—to coast down the hill on makeshift sleds in winter or play ball in spring and summer.

And after school, if Maud wasn't paying an "approved" call on Amanda or Penzie, she would spend a happy afternoon with Well and Dave, exploring their favourite haunts. One summer they built a playhouse in the spruce grove, carefully constructed in a circle of tangled trees, branches laid in to close the gaps between the leaves—complete with a door, fashioned of boards nailed together and held in place with leather hinges.

Slowly, slowly, Maud's constricted world was opening, while her imagination continued to thrive—and her writing as well. "I cannot remember the time when I was not writing or when I did not mean to be an author," she recalled in "The Alpine Path." By the time she was twelve, she had written "yards of verse about flowers and months and trees and sunsets"—despite her father's discouraging remarks about her earlier efforts, despite rejections of her best-loved creation (highly praised by the demanding Miss Robinson), a long poem called "Evening Dreams." Its simplicity is striking, as this stanza shows:

> *I forget the present and the future,*
> *I live over the past once more,*
> *As I see before me crowding*
> *The beautiful days of yore.*

The Last of the Marco Polo

The sea permeates all of Lucy Maud Montgomery's writing, as it filled her life even when she was physically distant from it. Drawn as surely to the forests, fields, and streams of her Island home as to its rocky red shores, she re-creates the beauty of the Cavendish countryside in an enchanting and powerful evocation made all the more believable by the unmistakable salt tang that drifts down the dustiest little lane.

Much of *Anne* is set in what Maud called the "green seclusion" of the land itself; but on the Island you're never far from the sea, and it only takes a few well-placed words here and there for a writer as skilled as Montgomery to make an indelible impression of its strong and lasting influence. For years before visiting Cavendish, I would dream of seeing the shore road as Anne did, bound for White Sands with Marilla, not knowing if she would ever return to Green Gables—yet unable to resist the rapture inspired by what she saw:

> *On the right hand, scrub firs, their spirits quite unbroken by long years of tussle with the gulf winds, grew thickly. On the left were the steep red sandstone cliffs, so near the track in places that a mare of less steadiness than the sorrel might have tried the nerves of the people behind her. Down at the base of the cliffs were heaps of surf-worn rocks or little sandy coves inlaid with pebbles as with ocean jewels; beyond lay the sea, shimmering and blue, and over it soared the gulls, their pinions flashing silvery in the sunlight.*

On just such "sandy little coves" Maud spent the summers of her childhood and youth, sometimes alone, later with Well and Dave, or Amanda and other school friends. The youngsters would watch the boats go by, comb the beach for pebbles and mussel-shells, and clamber up and down through the unbelievable soft sand of the dunes.

Grandfather Macneill kept a fishing boat at the beach and hired fishermen in the summertime; at three in the morning the men headed out to get mackerel, and at eight the children went down to the shore to take them breakfast. Maud, Well, and Dave always hoped for endless days of good fishing, so they would be able to enjoy the privilege of delivering the fishermen their dinner and supper as well. And afterwards, they could run up and down the long, sandy beach searching for more shells—or even pirate gold.

The summer that Well and Dave came to live at the Macneills', the three children were part of a seafaring adventure that didn't have to originate in their imaginations. It was in July of 1883 that the Norwegian-owned barque *Marco Polo,* then the fastest sailing vessel of her class ever built, sprang a leak in a terrible windstorm that had been slamming the Cavendish coastline for two days. The *Marco Polo* had apparently been in rough shape even before she began her voyage from England, bound for Canada to collect a load of deal planks; but on the return trip she became so waterlogged that her captain decided to deliberately run her aground to save his men and the ship's valuable cargo.

Captain P.A. Bull of Christiania (now Oslo), Norway, obviously knew his business: as the furious north gale drove him on, he ordered every sail opened fully, in order to drive the vessel into shore; she shuddered to a stop about three hundred yards out, and as the crew set anchor down and cut the rigging, the masts came hurtling down with such a crash that the students at Cavendish school sprang up from their desks in amazement.

By morning, the storm had sufficiently abated for the crew of twenty

This lovely scene of vivid red cliffs and blue sea and sky could shift suddenly into the sombre tints of a summer storm. Maud witnessed one of Cavendish's worst gales in 1883, when the famous *Marco Polo* ran aground.

to be brought ashore, tired, hungry, cold, and the object of the excited curiosity—and generous hospitality—of most of the residents of Cavendish, including Maud and her young friends. Grandfather Macneill invited Captain Bull to stay at the farmhouse while salvage efforts were being organized, which meant not only the delight of playing in the barnyard amidst "huge cables, as thick as a man's body," but also the entrancing sounds of just about every language imaginable, from Dutch to Tahitian—the crew members "haunted" the old farmhouse to confer with their skipper. The Macneills' dog, Gyp, earned three new names in the process, Maud later recalled: "The Norwegians called him 'Yip,' the irritable little German termed him 'Schnip' and an old tar twisted it into 'Ship'."

But the best part came the day Maud, Well, and Dave crept into the parlour to find the big table literally heaped with sovereigns of gold—a king's ransom, it seemed. Or maybe a glimpse of that pirate gold at last? To the children, the Tahitian sailors, at least, looked very much like pirates, for they wore gold earrings. The explanation, alas, was much more prosaic: Captain Bull was paying off his crew before their departure. The *Marco Polo* was sold, and the Macneill household returned to normal.

At least for awhile. Weeks of work and eighteen schooners were required to unload the cargo of deal, and a terrible August gale—worse than the storm in which the *Marco Polo* went aground—put the death-blow to the famous vessel. Worse, one of the men on the crew that had been unloading her was killed while he and two others were trying to get to shore.

Long, long after the wreck of the *Marco Polo,* the beach was strewn with her wreckage, and fishermen plying the waters could glimpse the shadows of her chains and anchor.

What a wealth of material for a future writer! Eight-year-old Maud, with her remarkable retentive abilities and pack-rat propensity for recording experiences, placed all the precious details in her memory bank (or her little diary). She would not be ready to give them full play in story or poem for some time, but she knew she *had* to keep hold of them, these memories more valuable than a king's ransom.

And in the meantime, what a wealth of material for three playful children whose imaginary voyages to foreign lands must have been even more exciting aboard those planks of wood from a real sailing vessel.

The sea is hidden from view in the dunes, but its presence is a certainty—as it is throughout Lucy Maud Montgomery's fiction, and her life.

Flowers of the Field

With the shift from childhood to girlhood came many changes in Lucy Maud Montgomery's life—as if she had not weathered enough already. When she was eleven, her friends the Nelson boys returned home unexpectedly—Maud was not even told about their departure before-hand. And soon after her twelfth birthday, she received a letter from her father telling her that he was intending to remarry in the spring: his bride-to-be, Mary Ann McRae, was from Cannington, Ontario, and the wedding would be held in the Presbyterian church there in April 1887. The future Mrs. Montgomery was in her early twenties when she and Hugh John were engaged—only twenty-four when they married—and she was strikingly lovely. She was also, apparently, quite domineering and demanding.

But the letter from Maud's father would have said none of this, of course, and Maud was delighted at the news. Perhaps she would know a mother's love after all! Her Aunt Annie Macneill was a wonderful mother to Uncle Leander's two sons, and she wasn't their "real" mother, so probably *her* new stepmother would be just as kind and loving. Maybe they could all live together someday, like a family, a *real* family.

I walk up through the sea grass and soft sand of a dune and into the fields around the Macneill foundation. The sound of waves echoing in their ancient pounding rhythms follows, as the landscape shifts from

Maud searched the fields for perfect flowers to press between the sheets of paper she filled with sweet messages to her new stepmother.

the blinding white and endless blues of sand and ocean and sky, to the myriad colours of the wildflower-strewn grasses of the field. I think of Maud, so hungry for a mother's love that she did not feel hurt about her father's remarriage. Certain that she would welcome her into the family, Maud began to write to her stepmother when the newlyweds returned to Saskatchewan later in the spring.

They were sweet, sentimental letters expressing Maud's happiness at their union and her fervent hope that she could at least visit them. In each letter she enclosed a wildflower—and oh! the flowers that abound here, the deep-hued wild violets of spring, the pale pink and pristine white roses that soothe the sea-sparked air with their sweetness, the girlish daisies and feathery purple or fuchsia-coloured lupine, the June bells, the lily-of-the-valley....How could Mrs. Montgomery have resisted their charm; plucked from their native soil and pressed between the pages of a letter, wouldn't they have prompted a smile, especially amidst those yearning, tender words?

But perhaps Mary Ann Montgomery, like Diana Barry's mother, was not inclined to keep an open heart. Just as Mrs. Barry persisted—despite Anne's assurances and apologies—in believing that Diana had been given currant wine *on purpose,* perhaps Mrs. Montgomery felt Maud was trying to ingratiate herself into a family she was not part of, and would never be part of.

Or perhaps she just didn't bother responding. At any rate, Maud did not record in her journals any assurances from her stepmother that her feelings were reciprocated; nevertheless she remained convinced that at some point there would be a joyous reunion with her father and a rewarding relationship with his wife.

A one room schoolhouse, faithfully preserved, circa 1895, Orwell Historic Village, Orwell Corners. "Comfortable substanial old fashioned desks" typical of Avonlea-Cavendish school-days.

I already know, as I stand here in the field drinking in the beauty of the wildflowers, that Maud will be disappointed when she finally meets her stepmother. Almost like Cinderella's, I think angrily, recalling the drudgery she would describe in her journal. But I also know that her capacity for love will survive, both in life and in her writing. She will, after all, see to it that Mrs. Barry relents and welcomes Anne back into Diana's life. She will cherish her own family, and her friends, and even the most difficult of her husband's parishioners (though not all to the same degree of fervour).

I bend to pick a perfect wild rose, a pale pink one, its petals more delicate than a swan's feather. It floats like down upon the gentle wind—then rose and reflections were gone.

Counting Stars

"I love Miss Stacy with my whole heart, Marilla. She is so ladylike and she has such a sweet voice....We had recitations this afternoon. I just wish you could have been there to hear me recite 'Mary Queen of Scots'....And Miss Stacy explains everything so beautifully. We have to write compositions on our field afternoons and I write the best ones."

Compositions, recitations, and a teacher who quickly became a "kin-dred spirit." Anne's Miss Stacy and Maud's Miss Gordon, who replaced Miss Robinson at Cavendish school the year Maud turned fourteen, might have been the same person. Kind, encouraging, and as dedicated to her students' physical and social well-being as to their academic develop-ment, she organized school concerts at the Cavendish Hall, and outings and picnics for them in spring and fall. Even the recalcitrant Macneills were no match for dynamic Hattie L. Gordon, who won their approval for their granddaughter to perform not only at school functions, but also for the local Literary Society.

Maud's first such recitation, of a piece called "The Child Martyr," was something of an ordeal. Like Anne confronted by the "professional elo-cutionist," Maud (presumably intimidated by all the literary ladies in the audience) had an attack of nerves despite the hours spent practising in front of her mirror. Somehow she got through, and Miss Gordon's praise was all the reward she needed.

Maud's writing efforts also blossomed under Miss Gordon's nurtur-ing approach. Her journal entries—she had been keeping a diary since the age of nine—continued apace. A story she wrote based on her grandfather's account of the Cape Leforce legend won honourable men-tion in the *Montreal Witness* school essay contest the first year Miss Gordon came to teach. And, closer to home, Maud started what was probably the first-ever literary workshop in the history of Cavendish school.

One summer day, as she, Amanda, and another friend were walking together, Maud hit on the idea that each of them should write a story based on the time-honoured theme of a tragic heroine who drowns herself. Shades of *Hamlet*'s Ophelia, perhaps—or, more to the point, a foreshadowing of the watery deaths of star-crossed Bertram and Geraldine, described glowingly by Anne and sighed over admiringly by Diana, whose complaint about lacking imagination is the spark that ignites Anne's Story Club.

Like Anne and her friends, Maud and her "workshop" members spent days—weeks—on their creative endeavours, enthusiastically discussing and criticizing each others' efforts afterwards. But for Maud, unlike her companions, this was no idle summer fancy, but serious practice for a budding writer—and the proof of the pudding would be the club's inclusion in *Anne of Green Gables*. In fact, the group has an entire chapter named after it!

Perhaps the most challenging literary project Maud undertook in her adolescence had its roots in an old school superstition: the first boy with whom a girl shakes hands after she has counted nine stars for nine consecutive nights is destined to be her future husband. (And, the ritual is reversible so that boys may count stars, too!)

Amanda and Maud had been trying since Maud's fifteenth birthday to count nine clear nights in a row, but the weather was not cooperating that year, and by February they *still* had not enjoyed success. Their

Beneath a maple tree in the woods behind Cavendish school, Maud sat down to read her first love letter.

friend Nate Lockhart, on the other hand, had apparently accomplished the mission before fall was out, and Maud, her curiosity inflamed beyond caution, agreed to the condition Nate placed on his agreement to divulge the desired information: she must answer a question in return.

Now, Nate and Maud had been school chums for quite some time. He shared her love of reading, and the two of them could often be seen together at recess, walking in the schoolyard and discussing the latest book they had read. Along with *his* best friend and desk-mate, John Laird, Maud and Amanda often joined forces with Nate in games of "Blind Man's Buff" on the school porch, or excursions to the shore.

Little did Maud know the friendship was anything more than, well, *friend*ship! Very much like Anne: "Boys were to her, when she thought about them at all, merely possible good comrades." But Nate, very much like Gilbert Blythe in other respects—serious, intelligent, gentlemanly— differed from his fictional counterpart in that he and Maud *were* friends, whereas poor Gilbert has to wait until the last few pages of the novel for Anne to forgive him over the "Carrots!" reference to her hair.

At any rate, Maud was surprised to learn she was the girl he had shaken hands with after counting the stars; and she was horrified by his question: "Which of your boy friends do you like best?"

What to do now? Of course I do like him best, but what if he should misinterpret my meaning? I just want to be friends! Oh, I know. I'll ask him the same kind of question about his girl friends. Of course he won't answer. And thus she reasoned to herself.

Well, he didn't answer—at first. But the next day, to her chagrin, Nate informed Maud that he would honour her request—which of course meant she had to answer too. In note form, of course.

Here's a sorry predicament, Well, no matter; she agreed. But would he go first? There was a long pause—why would he relish being in such a position any more than she?—but, gentleman that he was, Nate finally concurred.

So here's what, Maud told herself that night, sitting at the table in her little room, trying to write her note. *I'll give this to him if he says he likes me best, but not if he mentions one of the others.*

At last morning came; at last Miss Gordon gave Maud permission to go outside. She ran to her favourite spot, a big maple in the school woods, plunked herself down on the icy grass, and read, with growing horror:

Of all my feminine friends, the one whom I most admire, no, I'm growing reckless, the one whom I love (if the authorities allow the word to come under the school boy's vocabulary) is L.M. Montgomery, the girl I shook hands with, the girl after my own heart.

At dinnertime, expressionless, Maud passed her note to Nate through her French grammar book and went straight home; all afternoon she was cold and distant. In her diary that evening, she wrote that she was at once "triumphant" and "sorry"—someone really did care for her, "that way," but would it spoil their friendship? Carefully she recorded the date of her first *love letter:* February 18, 1890—just four days after Valentine's Day. And just what did this confession of love entail? A very Anne-like message:

> *You have a little more brains than the other Cavendish boys and I like brains—as I suppose I like you best—though I don't see why I should, after the trick you have played on me.*

The Competition

In writing an essay for the Witness *it is not my intention to relate any hair-breadth escapes of my ancestors, for, though they endured all the hardships incidental to the opening up of a new country, I do not think they ever had any hair-raising adventures with bears or Indians. It is my purpose, instead, to relate the incidents connected with the wreck of the celebrated "Marco Polo" off Cavendish, in the summer of 1883.*

Maud's essay on the wreck of the *Marco Polo* would be published twice—but Nate finished ahead of her in the *Montreal Witness* competition. And that was a hard one to swallow.

The opening paragraph of Maud's entry in the 1890 *Montreal Witness* school essay contest already bears the unmistakable stamp of her style—fluid, elegant, and alive with the subtle humour that would characterize her adult voice.

But what is even more remarkable about the essay is its strikingly rich detail, seamlessly woven into an account both visually stunning and rhythmically satisfying testament to her fine memory and acute ear for language. More than seven years after Captain Bull came to stay with the Macneills following the demise of the *Marco Polo,* Maud wrote of the event as if it had happened the day before—even though the reader already knows it did not.

Of the crew, brought ashore the morning after the vessel was run aground, she writes:

> *They were a hard-looking lot—tired, wet, and hungry, but in high spirits over their rescue, and, while they were refreshing the inner man, the jokes flew thick and fast. One little fellow, on being asked, "if it wasn't pretty windy out there," responded, with a shrug of his shoulders, "Oh, no, der vas not too mooch vind but der vas too mooch vater!"*

The "typical sea-captain" emerges as a "corpulent, bustling little man, bluff and hearty"; her recollections of the various mispronunciations of the family dog's name emerge complete, from "Yip" to "Ship," and the account of the fateful evening preceding the sinking of the *Marco Polo* strongly resembles descriptive passages in her adult fiction:

> *The sun set amid clouds of crimson, tinging the dusky wavelets with fire and lingering on the beautiful vessel as she lay at rest on the shining sea, while the fresh evening breeze danced over the purple waters. Who could have thought that before morning, that lovely tranquil scene would have given place to one of tempestuous fury?*

I stare out on the jutting red rock of Cavendish shore. The water is a deep blue, not purple—for it is afternoon—but the scene is as peaceful as Maud's description, and the breeze really *is* dancing. I can almost see the great barque out there, crippled but still magnificent, destined for a watery grave but never to be forgotten.

I smile a little ruefully, thinking of the essay contest. No, Maud did *not* win, though about a year afterwards, "The Wreck of the *Marco Polo*" was published—her first prose publication—in the *Mirror,* then reprinted in the Charlottetown *Daily Patriot.* Still in her mid-teens and already into second printings! That must have come as some consolation for placing third in the competition, a "defeat" made all the more ironic by the identity of the second-place finisher—none other than Nate Lockhart. The future lawyer had outdone the future best-selling author and, worse, it had to be the boy who played that "trick" on her during the star-counting episode.

Oh, well. Nate would get his comeuppance—in fiction, of course. It would happen near the end of *Anne of Green Gables,* as the Avonlea students anxiously await the results of the Queen's entrance examinations. The dreaded "pass list" seems to be an eternity coming; and finally, late one evening, Diana comes bursting into Anne's room, brandishing a newspaper:

> *"Anne, you've passed," she cried, "passed the very first—you and Gilbert both—you're tied—but your name is first. Oh, I'm so proud!"*

First among two hundred competitors—Anne Shirley, teacher-to-be. Yet I wonder, gazing out at the gleaming waters that Maud described so vividly in "The Wreck of the *Marco Polo*," how many among two hundred—or two thousand—would have been gracious enough to award their opponent a draw in the rematch?

The Mayflower Picnic

> *Away up in the barrens, behind Mr Silas Sloane's place, the Mayflowers blossomed out, pink and white stars of sweetness under their brown leaves. All the schoolgirls and boys had one golden afternoon gathering them, coming home in the clear, echoing twilight with arms and baskets full of flowery spoil.*

Simply change the name Silas Sloane to Charlie Simpson, and the favourite springtime ritual of Avonlea's budding young men and women becomes a faithful portrait of Cavendish scholars taking pleasure in the honour of Miss Gordon's Mayflower Picnic—tea at the Simpsons' and

Maud gloried in the blooms of a springtime outing with her school friends—and she bestowed upon Anne the singular pleasure of attending a Mayflower picnic.

an enchanted afternoon picking the "pink and white stars of sweetness," then lounging under the firs on a moss-carpeted hill to weave their floral bounty into wreaths and bouquets.

Anne, awakening that charmed May morning in the land of Avonlea, rejoices in her first glimpse of the Snow Queen at her bedroom window; the cherry tree's luxuriant blossoming marks her first full year at Green Gables—"the turning-point in my life," as she tells Marilla after the day's festivities are over.

But for Maud, a universe away, in the Cavendish of May 1890, the Mayflower Picnic marked a bittersweet moment of transition—her last year in the community that had been home for all but a year of her life. As she prepared to join Amanda and Jack, Lucy and Nate, Emma and Mamie and the others on the flower-gathering expedition, Maud did not know if ever again they would sit together in all the sweet freshness of spring, crowning each other with mayflowers, singing with all the joy of young birds. One bird, at least, would be flying west before summer came to a close.

Maud had known for some months that she was moving to Saskatchewan in mid-August. Indeed, her father's invitation came as the fulfillment of a dream she had clung to, steadfastly, since Hugh John and Mary Ann Montgomery's marriage three years before. Her stepmother had still not responded to her flower-enwrapped letters—or, at least, her journals make no mention of a response—but Maud could have concluded that the demands of her stepmother's new family made correspondence impossible. And Maud was thrilled to learn that her half-sister, Katie, now two years old, was about to be joined by a sibling. A lovely house in a bustling prairie town, a long train journey—Maud had never been on a train—and, most importantly, the golden opportunity to be part of her father's new family.

Since winter she had been counting the days until her departure; she was enjoying all that the auspicious year had brought, it's true, but always with one eye cocked on the tracks ahead. And yet—and yet it is the striking similarity of Maud's last mayflower outing to Anne's version—right down to the old well in a mossy hollow near where the students are gathering the blossoms—that leads me to believe that at least part of Maud was sorry to be leaving her Island behind.

> "I'm so sorry for people who live in lands where there are no Mayflowers," said Anne. "Diana says perhaps they have something better, but there couldn't be anything better than Mayflowers, could there, Marilla?"

A year later, almost to the day, a very homesick Maud, while typically praising the natural wonders that surrounded her—in this case, the prairie landscape, especially its violets and "blue bell-flowers"—would write wistfully to her friend Penzie:

> I suppose the mayflowers are plenty now. They do not grow in this country but I wish they did.

Time and the Sea

I have visited Maud's beloved Cavendish—and Anne's Avonlea—three times, but I've never been there early enough to gather mayflowers as they did. But I shouldn't complain; my summer sojourns have given me ample opportunity to enter their worlds, and it has been an experience I feel privileged to have been granted.

Such is the beauty and spiritual grandeur of this enchanted isle and the remarkable sons and daughters of its history, that access to the sacred, which thrives in sites both natural and constructed, is always possible. So convinced am I of this power of place that I invite you, reading these words, to come here and find out for yourselves. All you need to take with you on your journey is an open heart. And a bit of imagination.

As for me, I'm going down to the beach. I want to be there well before sunset; Maud and Amanda are planning a walk on the shore this evening—she said so in her journal—and I don't want to miss them.

It's a lovely day, bright and fresh, and as I stroll the long expanse of white sand, I imagine a solitary figure at the water's edge, a serious-looking youth of about fifteen or sixteen; one foot scuffling a bit of seaweed, he glances towards the pathway. He's expecting someone…

Just then, two young women his age amble onto the beach, their long light summer dresses fluttering in the light wind. Soon the three

As the sun sank low, Maud, Nate, and Amanda sat talking quietly of past and future, endings and beginnings.

are chatting happily. Nate, Maud, and Amanda, talking about the past and future, successes and dreams, endings and new beginnings— a conversation that flows "soberly but not sadly," for these young people are so deeply in the moment of their experience of sea, sand, sky, and one another that regrets and sorrows could not possibly penetrate.

I stay where I am, listening to the cry of the gulls while the three friends sit down together on one of the sea-washed rocks. In only two months they will be parted—Nate is off to college and Maud to Prince Albert—but for now it's as if they will be together forever. Slowly the light shifts as they stare out to sea; slowly the sky darkens, and the water goes grey.

The sun sank in a low bank of black clouds, leaving a wake of rosy gold, while below the cloud ran a strip of fiery crimson, flecked here and there with tiny cloudlets of gold and scarlet.

Where Past Meets Future

The train station at Kensington, near Park Corner, is no more in the business of transporting passengers or freight than the one at Hunter River. But unlike the old Hunter River site, on which Anne's destination, Bright River, was based, Kensington still boasts an immaculate stone station-house with a gleaming CN engine out front. Here on the platform is where Maud, accompanied by Grandfather Montgomery, awaited the iron horse that would gallop them out to a place still rich with the frontier romance of the Old West—a place that, for the lovely young woman anxiously scanning the track, represented a new home.

Journeys are odd experiences, I reflect, imagining two figures on the platform—kindly-looking Senator Donald Montgomery and his fresh, vivacious granddaughter by his side.

Here is Maud, about to leave the only home she has known to travel more than halfway across the country on the promise of a life with the father who never created a family around her. Here is her beloved grandfather, unwilling to let her travel alone, prepared to share her arduous journey. And here am I, destined to fly even farther away in just a few days—back to California. Who really knows when any of us will return?

In a sense, the answers are simple. The Senator will return after a brief visit out west, and I'll be back as soon as I can afford it! As for Maud, she has—poetically speaking—left one foot planted in the "dear red soil" of the Island, in the form of a verse sequence on the old Cape Leforce legend told her by Grandfather Macneill and rendered into prose for the essay contest two years before. Three months after her arrival in Saskatchewan, the finished poem will be published back home in P.E.I., in the *Daily Patriot,* marking the author's first-ever publication as it commemorates the early days of the Island,

> When war's dark cloud hung threatening low
>   Above our fair Canadian land,
> And echoes of the troubled strife
>   Reached e'en our Island's quiet strand;
>
> And o'er our blue Saint Lawrence Gulf
>   Sailed many a plundering privateer,
> Defying law and right and force
>   In their piratical career.

By the time a copy of the *Patriot,* carrying her "first darling brainchild arrayed in black type," reaches the ecstatic Maud, she will already be regretting her decision to come to Prince Albert, where her stepmother will expect her to serve as unpaid nurse to the two children and, "in plain English," as she will say years later, "be Mrs. Montgomery's household drudge."

Grandfather Montgomery and Maud left from Kensington station, bound for Saskatchewan, where Maud faced an uncertain future with her father and his new family.

A year after her departure, she will be back in Cavendish, and a whole new chapter in her life will be starting. And another, and another...

But as we stand here on the platform of Kensington station, none of us knows what the future will hold—not Maud and her grandfather in the summer of 1890, nor I in a summer more than a century later. This place of journeys is all about possibility, about past and future meeting in the eternal now. That is why we are here together—though we could be anywhere tomorrow, we're here now, and a part of us always will be. Here, or in the school hollow under the maple tree, or out in the fields behind the old homestead—

Or at Bright River station, sitting on a pile of shingles at the end of a long platform, scared but excited, waiting for someone named Matthew Cuthbert to take us home to Green Gables.

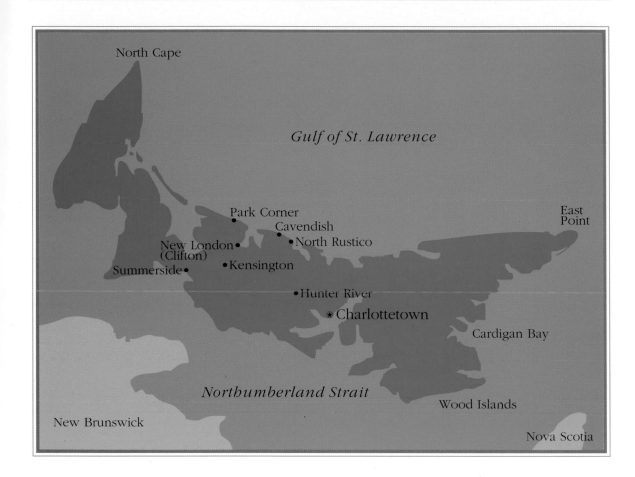

North Cape

Gulf of St. Lawrence

East Point

Park Corner
Cavendish
New London •North Rustico
(Clifton)
•Kensington
Summerside•

•Hunter River
✹Charlottetown

Cardigan Bay

Northumberland Strait

Wood Islands

New Brunswick

Nova Scotia

Map of Prince Edward Island

Charlottetown: capital of the province and the place where Anne's Boat Train arrived at Prince Edward Island from the Nova Scotia orphanage.

Hunter River: where the train station once stood and the model for Anne's Bright River Train Station.

Cavendish: Green Gables, Lovers' Lane, the Haunted Woods, and the Macneill homestead where Maud grew up.

New London: once known as Clifton, where Maud was born.

Park Corner: Grandfather Montgomery's homestead and the Campbell Cousin's homestead. Also known as Silver Bush.

Kensington: train station where Maud and Grandfather Montgomery headed west to Prince Albert.

Summerside: where Maud and Grandfather's Boat Train left Prince Edward Island, travelling west to Saskatchewan.

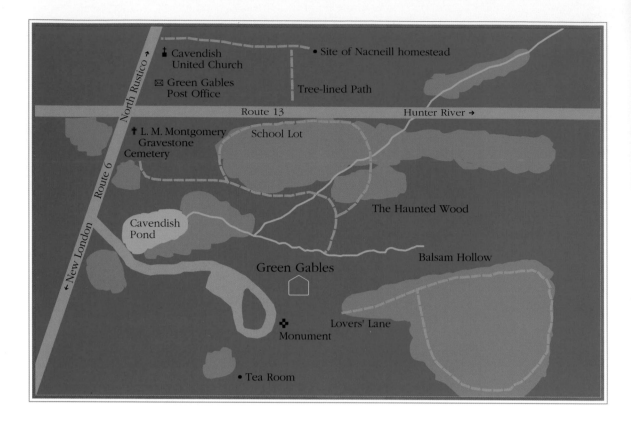

MAP OF CAVENDISH

Cavendish Pond: Maud wrote that the effects of light and shadow on these waters "figured unconsciously" in her description of the Lake of Shining Waters.

Green Gables: a real home built in the mid-1800s; owned by elderly cousins of Maud's.

Lovers' Lane: discovered by Maud in her childhood, it leads into Balsam Hollow, babbling brook, and old log bridge.

Balsam Hollow: this and all the other enchantingly lovely places around Green Gables were a fairy-tale playground to young Maud—and she never outgrew them.

The Haunted Wood: created by the imaginations of Maud and her friends, Well and Dave.

The Old School Site: where the one-room schoolhouse once stood. Located directly across the road from the path leading to the Macneill homestead.

The Tree-lined Path: extends from the Macneill's to the school lot.

The Macneill Homestead: only a stone foundation remains.

Cavendish United Church: formerly the Presbyterian church where Ewan MacDonald, Maud's husband, was once minister.

Cavendish Cemetery: gravesites of Lucy Maud Montgomery and her mother, Clara Woolner Macneill.

BIBLIOGRAPHY

Bolger, F. W. P. *The Years Before "Anne."* Charlottetown: Prince Edward Island Heritage Foundation, 1974; Halifax: Nimbus Publishing, 1991.

Gillen, Mollie. The Wheel of Things: *A Biography of L. M. Montgomery.* Toronto: Fitzhenry, 1975.

Montgomery, Lucy Maud. *Anne of Green Gables.* Boston: L. C. Page, 1908.

———. *The Alpine Path: The Story of My Career.* 1917. Toronto: Fitzhenry, 1975.

———. *My Dear Mr. M: Letters to G. B. Macmillan.* F. W. P. Bolger and Elizabeth Rollins Epperly, eds. Toronto: McGraw, 1980.

———. *The Selected Journals of L. M. Montgomery, Volume I: 1889-1910.* Mary Rubio and Elizabeth Waterston, eds. Toronto: Oxford University Press, 1985.

———. *The Selected Journals of L. M. Montgomery, Volume II: 1910-1921.* Mary Rubio and Elizabeth Waterston, eds. Toronto: Oxford University Press, 1985.

———. *The Selected Journals of L. M. Montgomery, Volume III: 1921-1929.* Mary Rubio and Elizabeth Waterston, eds. Toronto: Oxford University Press, 1992.